I0132038

William Fraser

Words on Wellington

William Fraser

Words on Wellington

ISBN/EAN: 9783337142742

Printed in Europe, USA, Canada, Australia, Japan

Cover: Foto ©Andreas Hilbeck / pixelio.de

More available books at **www.hansebooks.com**

WORDS ON WELLINGTON

THE DUKE—WATERLOO—THE BALL

WORDS ON WELLINGTON

THE DUKE—WATERLOO—THE BALL

BY

Sir William Fraser, Baronet

M.A. CHRIST CHURCH, OXFORD

LONDON

JOHN C. NIMMO

14, KING WILLIAM STREET, STRAND

1889

THE DUKE.

FREQUENTLY as I have heard the subject discussed, I never have known it finally settled as to who would have commanded at Waterloo, if the Duke of Wellington had been killed. The following bears upon this point. The Duke was always reticent on the subject of his intentions; even toward those with whom he was most intimate. He had not said a single word on this subject before the Battle of Waterloo to Lord Anglesey, then Lord Uxbridge, commanding the Cavalry. Late on the 17th of June Lord Anglesey called upon Sir Hussey Vivian, who commanded a Brigade of Light Cavalry under him. He said "I find myself in a very difficult position. A great battle will take place to-morrow. The Duke, as you know, will not economize his safety. If any accident happens to him I shall suddenly find myself Commander in Chief. Now, I have not the slightest idea what are the projects of the Duke.

B

I would give anything in the world to know the dispositions which, I have no doubt, have been profoundly calculated. It will be impossible for me to frame them in a critical moment. I dare not ask the Duke what I ought to do." Sir Hussey Vivian replied " Consult Alava. Perhaps he will take it upon himself to speak to the Duke." Count Alava was, as is well known, the Duke's friend and confidant during the Peninsular War; a Spanish officer of high rank; and of still higher character; for whom the Duke, to the end of his life, entertained a warm friendship; offering him, among other things, a residence near Strathfieldsaye. Lord Anglesey followed the advice; and, going to head-quarters, soon found the Spanish General: " I approve of your idea," said Alava, so soon as Lord Anglesey had explained his fears. " The question is a very serious one ; but I do not feel that I know the Duke sufficiently intimately to ask him for explanations. This is your affair entirely ; but, if you wish, I will go and tell the Duke that you are here." Lord Anglesey hesitated for a minute : then decided to follow Count Alava. In a few moments he found himself in the presence of the Duke. He explained the motive of his visit with all the delicacy imaginable. The Duke listened to him quietly to the end ;

without saying a single word: and when he replied,
it was without impatience; without surprize; and
without emotion. He said calmly "Who will attack
the first to-morrow, I or Bonaparte?" "Bonaparte,"
replied Lord Anglesey. "Well," continued the Duke
in the same tone "Bonaparte has not given me any
idea of his projects: and as my plans will depend
upon his, how can you expect me to tell you what
mine are?" Lord Anglesey bowed: and made no
reply.

The Duke then said, rising; and at the same time
touching him in a friendly way on the shoulder;
"There is one thing certain, Uxbridge, that is, that,
whatever happens, you and I will do our duty."

He then shook him warmly by the hand: and Lord
Anglesey bowing, retired.

There is no doubt that Picton joined the campaign
of 1815 with reluctance. He had told the Duke that
his health was such that he did not consider himself
fit to undertake the anxious task of commanding a
Division; and it was only at the earnest personal
solicitation of the Duke that he joined the Army.
He was, I believe, killed, wearing plain clothes; so
hurried had been his departure from London.
Severely wounded at Quatre-Bras, he concealed the

fact ; which was only known after his death. I heard many years ago, on good authority, that a Commission was found on Picton's person, giving him the absolute command of the British forces, and their Allies, in case of the Duke's death. This seems to me to be a very interesting question ; and should, if possible, be cleared up.

Whatever may have been Lord Anglesey's merits as a Commander of Cavalry, the anecdote related above reflects credit upon him. He must have felt conscious that he had never had the experience of commanding an Army ; and his position would have been an impossible one, had the Duke been killed.

The careful mind of the latter must surely have provided for this contingency. He thought it necessary, in the interests of the army which he commanded, to expose himself incessantly during the battle : and must have been conscious that at any moment a tremendous responsibility might fall upon another. Who that other would have been is a question worthy of inquiry, in the interests of History.

ONE OF THE EARLIEST occasions on which I saw the Duke of Wellington was a memorable one.

It was at the Funeral of his brother in the Chapel, when I was a boy at Eton.

When the Duke received the news of Lord Wellesley's death, he closed the letter, saying "There is a great man gone" : he then retired from the breakfast-table : and did not reappear during that day. I believe that this happened at Walmer.

Lord Wellesley had expressed an injunction in his will that he should be buried at Eton. This, in itself, was a pathetic incident. The man of surpassing intellect, the brilliantly successful Statesman felt, we may assume, that his earliest associations were the happiest; and wished to lie in the place where his sense of enjoyment had been keenest. The usual Morning Service was held previous to the Funeral; and at this were present, probably for the first time, all the brothers : the head of the family lay in his coffin ; his brother Lord Maryborough who, by Lord Wellesley's death, had become Earl of Mornington ; the Duke of Wellington ; the Revd Gerald Wellesley, and Lord Cowley sat together in Upper Stalls ; that is, on the Provost's side ; the boys, who usually sat there, having left them vacant for the occasion. The coffin on trestles was placed in the central aisle of the Chapel. At Morning Service,

choral, which was not usual, Lord Mornington's anti-
phonal chant, composed by the father of this illustrious family, was used for the Psalms. The Pall-
bearers were Lord Henley; Lord Belgrave, now
Duke of Westminster; the Earl of Darnley; Lord
Burghley, now Marquess of Exeter; Lord Dunkellin,
(dead); and Lord Robert Cecil, now Marquess of
Salisbury. After Morning Prayer the Funeral Service followed. Always impressive, that beautiful
composition never can have been more so than on
this occasion. What associations crowded on the
mind! I cannot imagine any of the boys insensitive
enough, and I think none were, not to be deeply
moved by what took place. No one who was there
could ever in the course of his life have forgotten it.
The coffin was slowly moved towards the grave,
which was near to the steps rising from the ante-
chapel into the chapel; and to the west of what was
then the organ gallery.

At the conclusion of the service the boys filed out.
We passed to the right of the grave, and, though
many years have elapsed, I can see now the Duke
standing alone on the left side of his brother's grave;
looking down into it. His upper lip quivered. This
I observed distinctly: and his arms were folded. The

boys descended to the school-yard; and thence into
'Long Walk': taking it for granted that the Duke
would come out that way. It would, of course,
under such circumstances have been unseemly to
cheer him : and yet, what Eton boy that ever saw
him did not long to do so? I calculated that he
would do all he could to avoid this; and my sur-
mises turned out to be quite correct. Going down
into the school-yard with the rest of the boys, instead
of turning into 'Long Walk,' I passed through
Lower-School passage ; turned to the left; and waited
alone near the door of Chambers ; close to the gate
of Weston's Yard. In a few minutes, as I expected,
the Duke emerged alone, having passed from the
Chapel through the Upper School, the Flogging-
room, down the stairs, into the Head-master's Chambers ; and thence out. He at once stepped into one
of Dotesio's crimson britzskas; and drove off to
Slough; no boy, but myself, saw him. I ought
perhaps to be proud of having circumvented even the
Great Duke.

The following Latin lines are an Epitaph written
by Lord Wellesley on himself and placed in the
hands of his old friend D⟨r⟩ Goodall, for many years
Provost of Eton.

" Fortunâ rerum que vagis exercitus undis
    In gremium redeo, serus, Etona tuum :
Magna sequi, et summæ mirari culmina famæ,
    Et purum antiquæ lucis adire jubar,
Auspice te didici puer ; atque in limine vitæ
    Ingenuas veræ laudis amare vias.
Siqua meum vitæ decursu Gloria nomen
    Auxerit, aut siquis nobilitaret honos,
Muneris, Alma, tui est : Altrix da terra sepulcrum !
    Supremam lacrymam da ! memoremque mei."

                        WELLESLEY.

Kingston House,
    January 5, 1842.

Tossed on the stormy waves of Fate,
Eton ! I seek thy breast, though late :
To hope to climb the heights of Fame,
To tend of classic lore the flame,
'Twas here I learned : and, in Youth's days,
To seek the paths of honest Praise.
If Glory shines upon my name,   .
Eton ! to thee I owe my Fame :
Of thee, sweet Nurse ! one boon I crave :
May Eton weep above my grave !

                        W. F.

Lord Wellesley was originally at Harrow.

Great excitement was caused in that school by an Eton man being appointed Head-master. Almost every boy joined in the uproar: and they were headed by the future Governor-General of India. Lord Wellesley either to set an example of prowess, or, moved by a deep feeling against Eton in general, threw a stone with fatal effect at the window of the carriage by which the obnoxious intruder entered Harrow.

An early, and Poetic retribution overtook him.

Removed from Harrow ; he was immediately sent to Eton ; where, as we know, he rose to great distinction.

I ASKED the Duke of B., a relation of the Duke, which portrait his family considered the best. The Duke replied "The one ringing the bell." He explained ' that he meant by this the picture in which the Duke is holding the Sword of State in his right hand; St. Paul's Cathedral is in the background : the scabbard looks not unlike an old-fashioned bell-pull. This portrait of the Duke in full uniform, Field-Marshal's coat, white leather pantaloons, Hessian boots with gold edging and tassels, and wearing the Orders of the

Garter, the Golden Fleece, Maria Theresa, Tower and
Sword, and the sash of a Captain-General of Spain,
was, I have no doubt, painted by Sir Thomas Lawrence
with great care. When, as he occasionally was,
inspired by his subject, Lawrence ceased to be commonplace. His portraits of Lord Castlereagh, in
Windsor Castle, and of his brother the 3rd Marquess
of Londonderry, bearing a sword on his shoulder,
are very fine.

I WAS TOLD by the 2nd Duke of Wellington an
interesting circumstance in relation to this picture.
I mentioned to him what the Duke of B. had said;
and he replied "Well, I think he is right. The one
thing my father was vain of was that he was the only
man, to whom the Sword of State had been given,
who was able to carry it upright. Everyone else, the
sword and scabbard being very heavy, 'sloped' it on
the right shoulder: my father carried it upright: and
he insisted upon Sir Thomas Lawrence painting him
doing this. Sir Thomas did everything he could to
persuade him that, as a matter of Art, this would
never do; that the portrait of a man perennially
carrying a heavy sword from his wrist would eventually fatigue persons looking at the picture; in

short it was against all the canons of Art. After long disputes Sir Thomas affected to give in; and he has painted my father, who still held to the point, with his right elbow apparently resting on a cushion. If you look closely at the print, you will see that his arm does not rest upon the cushion; but this can only be discerned by minute examination."

THE DUKE had a large hand and a very powerful wrist. I have a note on this subject from the 2nd Duke, which I may add later in relation to the sword worn by the Duke in all his battles.

THE ORIGIN of a term rather frequent when I was at a private school has not, I believe, been traced. A very common form of derision in the streets was "What a shocking bad hat!" applied generally, as usual, when undeserved. The origin was this. When the first Reformed Parliament met, the Duke went to the Bar of the House of Commons, to inspect them. Expecting, of course, to be questioned; and knowing that his words would be repeated, the Duke was ready for the inquisition: when asked, on walking back to the House of Lords, what he thought of the new Parliament, he evaded responsibility by replying

" I never saw so many shocking bad hats in my life " :
Hence the popular saying.

DURING MY Parliamentary life, I have always observed that the hats and boots of M.P.s were far
inferior to those of the average of mankind. In the
first Parliament in which I sat, the only man really
neat in these respects was Sir Benjamin Hall. I
think Disraeli came next.

I believe that the practice of wearing the hat, as of
that of the Peers sitting by command when the Queen
reads her speech, originated, as these things do, in
good sense. Were it compulsory on the Peers to
stand; or on M.P.s to sit bare-headed, an easy and
safe insubordination might be shown at any time, by
the latter covering themselves, or by the former sitting
down unbidden.

MARVELLOUS AS a compilation of good sense as
are the Duke's Dispatches, they are, in addition,
models of style. Whether he wrote in English or
French, and in the latter he wisely avoided idiom,
they show his clearness of mind; and admirable
powers of expression. " Le style c'est l'homme " :
and in no one was this more conspicuous than in the

Duke of Wellington. The following was given to me by the late Lieutenant-Colonel Johnson of the Guards.

THE DUKE on one occasion wished a bridge to be constructed, or something of a similar kind, the duty of the Royal Engineers. The Officer, after examination, reported to the Duke that it could not be done. The Duke was displeased; and sent for another officer, a young man, attached to another Division of his Army. This officer performed what the Duke desired. The Duke put the following in "Orders": " He who in War fails to do what he undertakes, may always plead the accidents which invariably attend military affairs : but he who declares a thing to be impossible, which is subsequently accomplished, registers his own incapacity." His splendid clearness of intellect gave him the power of expressing himself clearly: and, numerous as are his writings, hardly one can be found, the meaning of which is doubtful.

NO GREATER tribute could be paid to the lofty honour of the Duke than that shown by his enemies. Before the Battle of Orthez, the bridge over the

Gave de Pau, had been passed by the French army. The Duke sent a note to Marshal Soult, saying that a battle would, of course, take place on the following day; but that, as it was desirable in the interests of the inhabitants of Orthez not to destroy the bridge, he promised that, if Marshal Soult would abstain from blowing it up, no soldier of the British army should cross it. Soult trusted him: and the bridge is to this day intact. My father, Sir James Fraser, was at the time a Captain in the 7th Hussars, which formed part of Picton's Division. General Picton rode up to the regiment; and said "Surely some of you Hussars can find the way across that river: there must be a ford." My father accordingly, with a detachment of men, after some search, and under fire, discovered the ford and crossed it; the Division traversing the river in this manner later. It was at this battle that the Duke of Richmond, serving with his Regiment the 52nd, received a bullet, which remained in his body until his death.

I remember a remark of the same Duke of Richmond some years ago, at Gordon Castle. I thought it a wise one. He said "People talk nonsense about Lord Nelson being imprudent in wearing his stars at

Trafalgar. He was not shot because the man believed him to be Lord Nelson ; but, seeing him walk up and down the quarter deck, without a sword, and giving orders, he knew that he was a person of importance." I may point out here that the stars were not, as now, hooked on to the uniform by a brooch and pin ; but were in those days worked on the coat : and formed as much a part of the uniform as the embroidery on the collar.

Passing through Orthez some years ago, and naturally feeling very much interested, the following incident occurred, which I venture to give in its most condensed form :

DA-SHEALLADH.

(*Second Sight.*)

At ORTHEZ, one hot Summer's day,
When passing o'er the dusty way,
   That flanks the PYRENEES,
I stopped an hour; " LA BELLE HÔTESSE "
The Inn was called ; the Inn's maîtresse
   Wished, smilingly, to please.

" The room where the GREAT DUKE reposed
Pray show me."   Quickly she unclosed
    A door : " 'Twas there he lay."
" 'Twas 'mid the storm of shot and shell
That on your foot an Obus fell,
    The morning of the fray.

" Which is the cupboard, where the dinde,
Left by the diligence behind,
    Furnished the hero's supper ? "
" Here, Sir, it is ; forgive surprise ! "
" 'Twas on this shelf " (" Why, Sir, my eyes
    You open wide ! ") " the upper.

" ' We do not come to do you harm,'
He said ; then took you by the arm,
    I think it was the left."
" Sir has not numbered thirty years ;
Of speech, so wondrous this appears,
    I vow I am bereft."

" Nay, more than this, Madame, I know :
The day he crushed his country's foe,
    When hot from TOULOUSE fight

He bought for you a grey silk dress,
Which now your daughter does possess,
    And sent it the same night."

" 'Tis true Sir, all that you have said :
But how the Past you thus have read,
    In parting, tell me, pray ! "
" To me a second sight is given :
A SCOTSMAN I." " Protect me, Heaven ! "
    " Madame, a most good day ! "

I will only add that the excellent old lady, " La
Belle Hôtesse," was named BERGERAU ; that I have
not altered in the slightest degree what occurred ;
and that, should the intelligent reader wish for an
explanation beyond what is given, he or she may
satisfy their curiosity by the purchase of the second
edition of this book.

THE DUKE was asked which he, on the whole,
thought was the sharpest fight at which he had been
present. He said "That near Tarbes." This was
principally, I believe, fought by the Rifle Regiments ;
and is included in the generic term " Pyrenees."

WHETHER NAPOLEON ever entered his car-

riage after Waterloo is doubtful. He certainly left
the field on horseback : the route of his escape to
Charleroi was pointed out to me by M. Coulon, from
the Maison du Caillou on the Genappes road. He
was on horseback when he reached Charleroi ; and
his travelling carriage had been captured by the
Prussians; but whether he was in it shortly before
this capture I doubt. The carriage contained among
other things his swords : one is the sword alluded to
later in my letter to the " Daily Telegraph"; another,
a small straight sword with an eagle head, which I
have seen the Duke of Wellington wear when in full
dress. I believe that the dress sword of the Officers
of the Scots Greys, when dismounted, was made from
the pattern of this ; and, no doubt, was given to them
for the capture of the standard of the 45th French
Regiment. "Ces terribles chevaux gris! comme
ils travaillent," said Napoleon : and well he might.

I REMEMBER at a ball at Lord Wharncliffe's house
in Curzon Street, Madame Brunnow, for many years
the Russian Ambassadress in London, appearing with
a sort of pink velvet semi-circular cushion on the top
of her head ; in which many diamonds were fastened.
The Duke immediately walked up to her; and kissed

her on both cheeks. The old lady looked extremely delighted. I heard someone say " Madame, vous ne rougissez pas?" She replied " Au contraire ! J'en suis fière." The Duke, with his stern sense of duty, and total disregard of what ignorant people thought, walked on ; and Madame Brunnow then explained that on the Emperor of Russia's birthday, I think that was the occasion, everybody kissed everybody else ; so far as I could make out : at any rate everyone of a certain rank in society such as Dukes, Ambassadresses, etc. etc.

THE DUKE when visiting an Embassy, or in the presence of a Foreign Sovereign, always wore the first class of the Order which that Sovereign had given to him. I remember that, at the balls at the Russian Embassy, then at Ashburnham House, the Duke always wore the ribbon and star of the first class of the great Russian Order of St. George, the highest Military Order in Russia : he also possessing the Order of St Andrew, which is still higher in rank ; he preferred to wear the former for good reasons. I observed one day at Baden Baden the Emperor of Russia wearing the first class of this Order ; on my return to London, I asked Baron

Brunnow how it was that the Emperor of Russia was
permitted to wear this decoration ; the first class of
St George.   Baron Brunnow replied " What makes
you ask the question ? "   I replied " He has never
commanded an army of, I think, seventy thousand
men in a decisive campaign."   The Baron replied "I
will explain the matter to you.   You are quite correct
as to the statute of the Order ; but that was for
one hundred years only.   Two years ago the century
expired : and now our Emperor is permitted to wear
the Order."

The year before the war broke out between England and Russia, Baron Brunnow proposed to me to
accompany him to St Petersburg.   He was about to
pay the fatal visit that brought on the War in the
Crimea.   He had a place free for anyone to accompany him in the Malle Poste.   I have often deeply
regretted that I did not accept his offer.   His honest,
but bad advice to the Emperor Nicholas, and the
wretched expedition of the Peace Society, did all the
mischief.   Sir Hamilton Seymour, then Ambassador
at St Petersburg, told me that the Emperor Nicholas
would not believe till the last moment that a shot
would be fired ; and Lord Aberdeen, the British
Prime Minister, very shortly before the outbreak

told a relation of mine, who was in Parliament, that he might safely go to Rome for the winter with his family, " for there will be no war." Fatal words !

THE FOLLOWING has been told over and over again ; but incorrectly. I have ascertained lately from Lord D. and D., that this version is absolutely correct. He says that, coming from Newmarket, Thomas 2nd Lord Wilton, well known as an Author of Hymns ; the hero of " The Tommiad," by Lord Winchilsea ; told him among other stories about the Duke, with whom he was very intimate, what really occurred. The Duke was having his portrait painted, a practice he disliked, but submitted to. On one occasion he said " They have painted me in every attitude ; except standing on my head." The painter was Pickersgill. Finding the Duke getting rather drowsy under the operation, he wished to excite his attention ; and thus give some expression to his face. He succeeded only too well. Pickersgill said " I have often wished to ask your Grace a question." The Duke was far too prudent to say " What is it ? " Pickersgill then said " Were you really surprized at Waterloo or not ? " The Duke instantly replied " No ! but I am now." I am not sure that Lord

Wilton was not at Walmer at the time : he was frequently the Duke's guest at the Castle.

ON ONE OCCASION at Walmer the Duke found himself in an embarrassing position ; but even here his mental resources did not fail him. He found himself shut into a very small room indeed : and, by an accident to the bolt, he failed to open the door. This very small room had a very small window, through which it was possible to see horizontally ; but, from the thickness of the castle wall, not vertically. Few would, I think, have known what to do. It would not have been well for the Duke to rouse the neighbourhood by shouts ; for those shouts would have reverberated throughout the civilized world ; and every sort of story of illness, and death would have circulated. The Duke retained the same calmness as he did in battle. Opposite to the window was a tower deeply covered with ivy. In this ivy the Duke had observed that starlings were in the habit of nestling. He accordingly waited ; and no sooner did the little birds fly out in a mass, than the Duke concluded that some human being was passing. He then called out : and was liberated.

ON THE MEMORABLE occasion of the Duke's ride through London, on the 18th of June, 1832, he had been to the Mint: on his return he wished to visit Sir Charles Wetherall in Lincoln's Inn. The Liberal Party in London had got scent of his arrival on Tower Hill; and were determined to give him a "Charivari" on his way home. Most of the particulars of his ride are well known: but I may mention that the gentleman in a gig, who helped to protect him in East Holborn, and who disappeared, without giving the Duke his name or address, when he arrived at Lincoln's Inn, was ultimately known. The Duke made every exertion to find him at the time by advertisement; but failed. Many years afterwards a gentleman sent his card up to the Duke at Apsley House; and the latter saw him. The Duke asked him what his business was: and he replied, that his Grace might remember that many years before he had been of some slight service to him in Holborn. The Duke expressed his great delight at seeing him; and asked if it were possible for him to be of any use to the stranger. The latter replied that he had a very small favour to ask on behalf of some individual, which the Duke instantly granted; and expressed his regret that the favour asked for

was not greater. On the day in question, after leaving Lincoln's Inn he proceeded along the Strand, and
Pall Mall. When passing the United Service Club,
the windows of which were, of course, lined with
members, the Duke looked straight between his
horse's ears. I had this from Lord St Germans, who
happened to meet him. He turned his horse; and
rode with the Duke through the Park gates near Stafford House, and up Constitution Hill, the mob at the
same time rushing across the Green Park, in order
to intercept him at his own door. The Duke said
but little on the road; but passing through the
crowd, which he did without the slightest hesitation, when the door of his house was reached, he
touched his hat to Lord St Germans; and quietly
said, " An odd day to choose ! " (Waterloo day).
" Good morning."

The Duke would not have the windows of Apsley
House repaired; he had iron shutters placed; the
interior window being at night covered with large
plate-glass sliding mirrors. He felt, no doubt, that his
house might at any time be attacked; and that these
shutters would be à good protection : but the reason
for not mending the windows was not, I believe, due
to his wishing to keep them as a memorial of this

atrocious outrage ; but because the Duke held that, in cases of public riot, the "Hundred" was bound to make good the loss. Familiar, as he was, with the history of the "Great Book," he may on that afternoon have thought of One who was received with the wildest shouts of "Hosannah to the Son of David": and, a little later was surrounded by the same vile wretches crying "Crucify him ! Crucify him ! "

Some years afterwards, when the Duke was at the height of popularity, a great crowd waited in Piccadilly; and gave him a tremendous ovation on his return home. The Duke took not the slightest notice of their cheering; but, just previously to entering his gates, he pointed with his right hand calmly to the iron shutters. He then took his hat off, with a mockery of gratitude ; and entered his house.

I saw, after his death, the windows being mended : every pane without exception on the Piccadilly side was smashed.

A RIBBON AND MEDAL were given eventually to the survivors of the Peninsular War; after too many brave men had passed away. I observed that the Duke wore the second ribbon, which differed very slightly from that given for Waterloo, attached also to the Waterloo medal : one bright the other faded.

THE DUKE was mindful of the oath which he had taken when made a Knight of the Garter, always to have some insignia on his person. In this, as in other things, he was a lover of truth.

The popular idea that the only civilians who have a right to hoist the "Union" flag over their house are Lords-Lieutenant of Counties, is a mistake. Knights of the Garter have the right; no doubt as the sequence of the permission to hoist the white banner of S[t] George, before the "Union" flag was invented.

THE DUKE received, almost without exception, the first class of every European Order. The principal ones, the Golden Fleece of Spain, the S[t] Esprit of France, S[t] Andrew of Russia, the Black Eagle of Prussia, the Elephant of Denmark, he had no difficulty, of course in discriminating; but, when it came to the minor States, he was sometimes puzzled. On one occasion, being asked to meet at dinner at Windsor Castle a second class Crowned Head, the Duke, who carried his orders with him in a lined box, could not recollect, among so many, which was the Grand Cross of the particular Sovereign. Accordingly he desired his servant to consult the valet of the distinguished personage in question. Either by the maladroitness of the Duke's servant, or more probably of the servant of the foreign Prince, the Duke's drawer of Orders was carried up to the latter; no doubt to his disgust.

THE DUKE being asked whether he found much advantage in being a great man, and having a completely acknowledged position, besides his wealth, and political power, said "Yes; I can afford to do without servants: I always brush my own clothes: and if I were strong enough, I would black my own boots."

I HAVE AVOIDED, and shall avoid going into the question of the Duke's political career. The first Soldier, and the first Diplomatist in Europe, he knew little of home politics; and he knew that he knew little. Circumstances, the principal of which was his high, unblemished character for honesty, forced him into a position for which he knew that he was unfit. The seven best years of his life, when Statesmen are learning, or ought to be learning, their duties, were passed in the campaigns of Portugal and Spain: and no one can have felt more acutely than the Duke how this absence of apprenticeship had unfitted him for his subsequent political career. He said so repeatedly: and he felt it. There are silly and shallow people who have said that the first dozen men passing through Temple Bar would make so good Cabinet Ministers as any others. Nothing more senseless ever came from human lips. It has been said that nothing more is required than Good Sense. Good sense is, of course, required in every art. No man can paint a picture without good sense. No man can amputate a limb without good sense. The total absence of this quality from the minds of those who utter such Twaddle is wonderful.

What is required to be a Cabinet Minister? It is Good Sense plus Experience: to suppose for a moment that a man of fifty can suddenly take up a science, and become master of what requires a life-time of observation, and an exceptional intellect, is absurd.

With our extremely complicated political system; with the endless variety, and constantly shifting opinion of the Houses of Parliament, who can possibly be of use, unless he has commenced his career at an early age? Find your most sensible friend: ask him if he will go to St George's Hospital, and cut off a man's leg. Would not your friend laugh in your face? Find another sensible friend, and ask him to paint an oil picture for the Exhibition next year: would not he do the same? Yet in an Art and Science which require more Genius than all the rest put together, we have been seriously told that the first man we meet in the street is as good as any other: and that any man of fifty, who is not an absolute fool, can govern a Kingdom. We all know Byron's irony .

"Critics all are ready made."

If this sarcasm applies to Criticism, possibly, in its loftiest sense, a higher art than Art itself, it is ten times more applicable to the mental condition of a Statesman.

THE DUKE SPOKE of the Reform Act of 1832, as a "Revolution in due course of law."

ONE OF THE MOST INTERESTING sights I saw while at Eton, was the Review of the Household Brigade, and Artillery, and one Regiment of the

Line, given by the Duke for the Emperor Nicholas
in Windsor Park.

The Review took place on the Eastern side of
Queen Anne's ride: the weather was perfect. A very
large Staff, and a vast number of Officers, Lords-
Lieutenant, and others, were present. The Life
Guards, and Guards, looked, as usual, splendid.
The Emperor had especially insisted upon seeing a
Regiment of the Line, "such as those with which
you win your battles in India." Accordingly the
47ᵗʰ Regiment was paraded. It being soon after
Montem, the last, we Fifth Form boys wore our
scarlet coats.

The Emperor was dressed in a dark green uniform ;
trousers of nankeen ; his boots round at the toes ;
black helmet, and cuirass, and gold epaulettes. He
rode very short. His features were different from
those of the Emperor Alexander ; whose portraits
had a retroussé nose, and a rather insignificant
face. The Emperor Nicholas had a fine Greek
face. Everything possible was done to receive him
with exceptional honour. The Knights of the Garter,
and other Orders, wore their ribbons ; and, what I
have never seen before nor since, Lord Combermere
and Lord Anglesey wore the Stars of the Bath and

Garter respectively, screwed to the cuirasses which they wore as Colonels of the 1st Life Guards and Blues. One incident occurred which brought down great vituperation upon the Prime Minister. When the Review was about half way through, Sir Robert Peel, who was then at the nadir of unpopularity in relation to his political conduct, cantered up into the midst of the large and brilliant group of uniforms, in plain clothes. He rode a handsome chestnut horse; and was dressed in a loose blue frock coat, yellow waistcoat, and drab trousers. He at once rode up to the Emperor Nicholas; made him a low bow; and, on the Emperor extending his right hand, kissed it. I may mention here that the Emperor drove through Eton on his way from Slough to Windsor Castle a few days before; while we were in three o'clock school. The false report spread that he was coming; and we were allowed to rush out to see him. It turned out to be only the King of Saxony; for whom the boys, by comparison, expressed great contempt. However a little later the Emperor passed. He was sitting in one of Dotesio's britzkas; alone; and on the edge of the seat. He struck me as a singularly handsome man; very tall; with very broad shoulders; but not very

well-bred. Being always in uniform, and holding
himself square, no doubt gave him this appearance.
I believe that it has always been reckoned the
pride of the British officer that, when out of uniform,
no one should take him for a soldier.

I recollect that in afternoon church at Eton on
the day of the Review a somewhat novel effect in
music occurred. The beautiful anthem " Holy,
Holy" was being sung in the chapel of Eton, and
one of the choristers, named Foster, who had an
extraordinary alto voice, was giving a very high and
prolonged note. At that instant a battalion of the
Guards returning from the Review crossed Barnes
Pool Bridge : the Band struck up, as it was bound
to do when leaving a town, " The girl I left behind
me." Anything so extraordinary as the effect of the
music reverberating through the chapel I have never
heard before nor since.

THE DUKE REMEMBERED no doubt what was
said to him who consulted the oracle at Delphi as to
how to achieve Immortality. " Go," said the Oracle
" and kill One already Immortal." We know that
he took the Oracle at its word; and murdered
Philip of Macedon.

Neither Napoleon, nor the Duke of Wellington, ever allowed anyone to shave them. The Duke performed this delicate operation with consummate skill: but declared that he never could get his servants to keep his razors in order. He was in the habit of taking a number of them at a time to a little cellar, subsequently a newspaper shop, in Piccadilly, close to the Burlington Arcade: he waited while they were sharpened.

Charles II. showed his astuteness on one occasion when his barber was at work on his head. This was at a time when full bottomed wigs were worn. The barber who was no doubt, like his master, fond of a joke, said, with a slight flourish of his razor, "I have often thought how completely I have got your Majesty in my power." Charles rose: and said good-humouredly, but decisively "You shall never shave me again: there is treason in the thought."

BRILLIANT AS were the abilities of the Duke he, like other great men, could not talk twaddle. He found no difficulty in speaking to children; whose naive manners, and originality of thought delighted him; but the wretched trash talked by grown-up children was to him intolerable. The story is well-known of his saying "I have no small talk; and Peel no manners."

We cannot fancy the Duke asking, even in a railway carriage, "Have you seen Salvini?" nor "Do you admire Mrs Langtry?"

THE DUKE'S whole nature was practical. Instead of considering, and theorizing, as to various arms, garments, belts, etc. worn by the British soldier, he sent for a man of a Line Regiment. Having provided a large pair of scales, he said to the soldier "Step into that scale with your musket, pouch, knapsack, schako etc." He had the weight written down. "Now then, get out; strip yourself naked; and then get into the scale again." That settled the question.

There is, or was, at the Clothing Department in Pimlico a quaint old Infantry schako. It bears Roman numerals on the front. With it was this memorandum: "The Duke of Wellington has worn this schako for seven hours to-day. He considers it an excellent head-dress for the soldier." Most men who have tried it on would be very sorry to wear it for seven minutes; and would differ with the Duke. However, "there were giants in those days."

I ASKED the 2nd Duke why it was that his father
always patronized the Ancient Concerts ; terrible per-
formances, which I attended once or twice in my boyhood. He replied " I will tell you why. My grandfather, Lord Mornington, was, as you know, a great
musician ; my father attended the concerts regularly,
because his father had either instituted or patronized
them." The Concerts were held at the Hanover
Square Rooms. I said that I had always noticed that
the Duke took care to sit between two handsome
women on the sofa which was placed in the front rank
for his special use. This may have consoled him for
what must have been to him severe suffering. He
had a dinner party at Apsley House ; and took, I
believe, his party to the concert.

THE 2ND DUKE told me the following story in
relation to the horse whose name will never die :
'Copenhagen.' The Duke gave a long price for him,
I think three hundred pounds. He was a hollow-
backed, powerful horse. Some years after the 1st
Duke's death, an old servant, who had served the
family for many years, came to him. He produced
something wrapped up in the " Times " newspaper ;
and, with hesitation, said " My Lord ; I believe that

I shall not live very long: I have come to place
in your Grace's hands what belongs to you." The
Duke naturally asked, with some surprize, what this
could be. The old man then slowly took out of the
parcel a horse's hoof. He said : " My Lord : when
Copenhagen was buried" (near Strathfieldsaye House)
"I cut off one of his hoofs. None of us imagined
that the Duke would trouble his head about the
body of the horse : but he walked down ; and saw
him buried. He instantly noticed that the hoof
was gone. He was in a most terrible passion ; and
no one dared to tell him what had happened. I
have kept the hoof carefully ever since : and now
I give it back to your Grace." I have often heard
when in the 1st Life-Guards, dining at St James's
Palace, regret expressed that, whereas the hoof of
Napoleon's horse ' Marengo ' was used there daily as
a snuff-box, the hoof of ' Copenhagen ' could not be
placed beside it.

I HAVE SAID that the Duke shaved himself. Here
is another remarkable indication of the good sense
which told him that, whereas he had always been the
butt of the slanderer, he remained the object of the
less cowardly assassin. An Officer in the Regiment

quartered in the neighbourhood, walked to Walmer Castle soon after the Duke's death. He asked his servant whether he could spare any article, however insignificant, of the Duke. The servant said " There are a lot of umbrellas in that corner ; if you like, you can have one of them." The Officer took up one of the umbrellas ; and endeavoured to open it. To his surprize he drew out a sword. He pointed this out : the servant replied "Oh, yes ; there is a sword in every umbrella." This, no doubt, would have given the Duke a chance, who walked about London, and elsewhere, absolutely unattended, had he been attacked.

THE DUKE being asked how it was that he had succeeded in beating Napoleon's Marshals, one after another, said " I will tell you. They planned their campaigns just as you might make a splendid set of harness. It looks very well; and answers very well ; until it gets broken ; and then you are done for. Now I made my campaigns of ropes. If anything went wrong, I tied a knot ; and went on."

WHEN ASKED what was the best test of a great general, he replied " To know when to retreat ; and to dare to do it."

TWO FRIENDS upon whom I could rely, both
General Officers, told me that, on separate occasions,
they heard the Duke say this.   He rarely spoke about
Waterloo ; but they heard him say, sweeping the table
with his closed hand " Had I had the army that broke
up at Bordeaux, I should have swept him off the face
of the earth in two hours."

ON SOME one saying " Do you think it true that
Habit is second Nature ? " he replied " Second Nature ?
it's ten times Nature."

THE 2ND DUKE said to me, when riding in Hyde
Park, " You told me some years ago that when
Napoleon heard of my father's first victory at Assaye,
he said ' That is the man with whom I shall have to
deal :' I would give a great deal to know where you
learned that." I replied that I could not tell him : but
that I was quite sure that I had heard it on some very
good authority.

AN ORIGINAL PORTRAIT of the Duke which
I have, wearing the Star of the 'Tower and Sword,'
of Portugal, without other decoration, was carefully
examined by the 2nd Duke at my chambers.   He
said " Has he given him a tusk ? "   I asked an

explanation. He said "He had at that time an over-hanging tooth from his upper jaw." I looked closely at the portrait; there was the tooth.

He told me at another time a very interesting fact in relation to the configuration of the Duke's face, which I shall give further on.

In the portrait named above by Dighton, 38th Regiment, the Duke wears a General's uniform, a handsome blue cloth plastron; with flat gold embroidery, now only seen on the uniform of the Master of the Horse; high blue collar; his scarlet coat slightly open at the waist, showing a scarlet waist-coat with gold edging; blue stocking-net pantaloons, well fitting Hessian boots, and spurs. The cocked hat with white edging and no plume is, I think, peculiar.

I have placed on the frame of this picture the lines altered from Lord Lytton, which I shall quote later.

THE DUKE used to say that he attributed his success, in some measure, to always being a quarter of an hour earlier than he was expected: and that the wise course, in Action, is to attack your enemy at the moment he is preparing to attack you.

I BELIEVE that everyone, who has achieved great

success, has, at some time of his life, staked everything
upon a card.

THE POPULAR IDEA encouraged especially by
his enemies, was that the Duke had plenty of solidity;
but no dash. Greater rubbish never was talked. His
circumventing Soult by passing his whole army across
the River Douro in three punts, certainly excelled in
dash anything that any French General ever did.

I believe the title of " Douro," a name by which he
was always, after this, saluted by the Spanish troops,
was dear to him. When created a Duke he took it as
his second title.

WHEN THE STARTLING news of Napoleon's
leaving Elba reached the Congress of Vienna, Talley-
rand said "Wherever he goes, he never dare enter
France." The Emperor Alexander turned to the Duke
of Wellington, and, placing his hand upon his shoulder,
said " C'est pour vous encore sauver le monde."

I HAVE HEARD from many, who were in public life
at the time, that the Duke's position after Waterloo was
not nearly so great as that which he subsequently
attained. He was then looked upon as a brilliantly

successful General. The facts, which placed him so
high as a diplomatist, were not then known : Lord
Castlereagh overshadowing him. His fame, and reputation, in the minds of those whose good opinion
is alone worth having, rose steadily. Every year of
his life increased his appreciation by wise, and honourable, men.

TWO GREAT OFFICERS are appointed for
special occasions only. These are the Lord High
Constable, and Lord High Steward of the Kingdom.
On the occasion of the Coronation of George IV. the
Duke was nominated to the function of Lord High
Constable. On either side of the Champion of England,
and adding greatly to the splendour of the function,
were the Lord High Constable, and the Deputy Earl
Marshal. When the Champion enters Westminster
Hall, during the banquet, he rides between these
two Great Officers from the principal door up to
the King's table ; the King being seated under the
window at the farther end. After the customary
challenge made by the King's Champion to anyone
who should dispute the right of the Monarch, and
the throwing down of the glove, the King drinks
to the health of the Champion in a goblet of gold,

which he there and then presents to him. This being done, it is the duty of the Champion, the Lord High Constable, and the Earl Marshal to rein their horses backwards, until their exit at the door by which they entered from Palace Yard.

The Duke, with his practical good-sense, anticipating the scene of tumultuous enthusiasm which was certain to occur, took care to obtain for the occasion a well-trained steed from the establishment across the river, since known as Astley's. Accordingly, an animal of handsome appearance, and dignified demeanour, was selected : and, a backward movement being unusual to horses, the steed upon whom so much honour was conferred was carefully drilled day after day for some weeks to move in an inverse direction round the Circus. In time he became quite perfect ; and equally insensible to the efforts made by persons employed to disturb his equanimity. No amount of cheering, nor throwing up of hats, nor noises of any kind induced the animal to swerve from his backward path.

The great day arrived. The King was in his seat. The Peers, and Peeresses, and everything that was great in the Kingdom had found their proper locality in Westminster Hall ; the noble building raised by

William Rufus (for his bedroom). The great doors
were thrown open; and a sight which eclipsed
all other sights enchanted the spectators. The
Champion of England in brilliant armour entered
between his supporters. Nothing could be more
imposing.

The Hero of Waterloo wearing his Coronation
Robes, his Ducal Coronet placed rather forward on
his brow, and bearing in his right hand the bâton of
a Field-Marshal, bestrode with great dignity his noble
steed, duly caparisoned for the occasion. The sight
was irresistible. The Peers, Peeresses, and com-
moners rose to their feet: a wild burst of cheering echoed through that vast, and picturesque roof.
What was the horror of the spectators; what was
the dismay of the Sovereign; and what must have
been the feelings even of that iron soul, that had
confronted death in every shape unmoved, when the
intelligent animal which he rode, assuming that the
noise was the preliminary to his turning round, as he
had been trained to do, instantly did this: and
advanced towards the Sovereign with his head pointing to the door by which he had entered Westminster
Hall. As children say at the end of a good story,
" What did they do then?" Some of those in atten-

dance with great difficulty succeeded, to use a
sailor's expression, in "slewing" the animal round;
and possibly by dint of holding the bridle, and
caresses, enabled the great Duke to approach
George the Magnificent, in a decorous, and dignified
manner.

My father, who was page to the Lord High Steward,
was present on this occasion; and Lord Lucan, who
only died in the autumn of '88, told me that he
walked up Westminster Hall with him; he, Lord
Lucan, being page to Lord Lauderdale carrying the
Great Banner of Scotland.

IT HAS BEEN SAID of George IV. that he asked
Sir Walter Scott pointedly whether he was the author
of "Waverley," or not. George IV. was much too well-
bred a man to do anything of the sort. What I have
heard happened was this. At the time, when it was
almost universally known who the Author in question
was, George IV., at a dinner at Carlton House,
looking at Sir Walter Scott, said "Mr Scott: I drink
to the author of 'Waverley.'" Scott replied "I will
take care that your Royal Highness's toast is conveyed to the Author." This, no doubt, originated the
silly, and slanderous story.

THE DUKE was a practical philosopher of the best sort. He says himself that he had been slandered from his boyhood; but no amount of Calumny ever induced him to swerve from the straight, and wise path. Of a far gentler nature than Frederick the Great, he partook of some of his qualities. Frederick, riding one day with his aide de camp, saw a crowd, collected in a by-street of Berlin, doing their best to read a placard posted rather beyond their sight. The King enquired what it was. His aide de camp replied " A scurrilous poster against your Majesty." " Oh," said Frederick " have it brought lower down at once: they cannot read it where it is." When Voltaire wrote to him, threatening all sorts of disclosures, he at once put his letter into the Official Gazette.

STAYING AT KNEBWORTH with the late Lord Lytton, we drove thence to Lord Salisbury's house at Hatfield. In the dining room are two portraits : at one end that of Charles XII. of Sweden, at the other that of the Duke. I said to Lord Lytton " If I were Lord Salisbury, I should write under that portrait (Charles XII.)

'A frame of adamant; a soul of fire;
'No dangers daunt him; and no labours tire.'

and, under this (of the Duke)

> ' He rose
> ' Without one thought that Honour could oppose.' "

Lord Lytton seemed delighted: and said, "You have improved my lines: you will see that I shall alter them."

I cannot resist to insert, although they are, or ought to be, familiar to every one, the beautiful description given by the 1st Lord Lytton of the Duke of Wellington in "The New Timon."

> " Next, with loose rein, and careless canter view
> Our Man of men; the Prince of Waterloo :
> O'er the firm brow the hat as firmly prest,
> The firm shape rigid in the buttoned vest :
> Within, the iron which the fire has proved :
> And the close Sparta of a mind unmoved!
>
>   *   *   *   *
>
> Warm if his blood; he reasons while he glows :
> Admits the Pleasure; ne'er the Folly knows.
> If for our Mars his snare had Vulcan set,
> He had won the Venus; but escaped the net.
>
>   *   *   *   *
>
> Yet oh ! how few his faults, how pure his mind
> Beside his fellow-conquerors of Mankind :

How Knightly seems the iron visage shown
By Marlborough's tomb; or lost Napoleon's throne !
Cold if his lips, no smile of fraud they wear:
Stern if his heart, still ' Man ' is graven there :
No guile, no crime his step to Greatness made :
No Freedom trampled : and no Trust betrayed :
The eternal ' I ' was not his law : he rose
Without one *art* that honour *might* oppose."

I asked Lord Lytton, on the same day, whether
some lines that I had found many years before, when
staying at Hatfield House, in a scrap-book, on the
" Amorino " in the Vatican, were not written by him.
He told me that they were not : but my recollection
of the style, and particularly of the handwriting,
induced me to suppose that he had written them ;
and forgotten the fact.

THE DUKE was perhaps the only great man we read
of, who was perfectly neat in his dress.   He was known
in Spain as " The Dandy "; not as a term of deterior-
ation : he was conspicuous, at a time when the British
Army was not well dressed, for the careful manner
in which he wore his clothes.   I never remember to
have seen him, in the morning, nor in evening Society,

but what he was a model of good taste in this respect.
I must not be understood to say that there was anything made up, or, as the French would say, "apprété."
He had the perfection of art; for whether dressed as
soldier or civilian, he looked as if his clothes naturally
fitted him well, if I may use the term.   In later years
he almost invariably wore a garment, then novel, and
known as a 'Paletôt,' single-breasted, straightly cut, and
reaching to his knees; with a narrow, turn-down, collar
of the same material as the coat; and buttoned rather
high up.   His hat always with a very clean lining of
pale yellow leather, had a narrow brim, trousers usually
of grey, or "Oxford mixture," as it was called; and
his boots or shoes well shaped, and well blacked: he
always carried two cambric pockethandkerchiefs.   On
the 1st of May, on which day all soldiers in uniform
had to wear white trousers, the Duke so appeared;
supplementing them, no doubt, by very thick drawers.
In the evening he wore, usually, a blue tailed coat,
with velvet collar, and handsome gilt pin-buttons;
sometimes a white waistcoat; sometimes a black one.
On great occasions black breeches, black silk stockings
and buckled shoes; of course with the 'Garter' below
the left knee.   On ordinary occasions, and in cold
weather, black cloth pantaloons, with the 'Garter'

tied over them; black silk stockings, shown at the ankle, and shoe-strings.

THE DUKE invariably wore, except in the presence of a Foreign Sovereign, or at a Foreign Embassy, across his waistcoat, only the Garter ribbon ; the Star of the Garter on the left breast of his coat ; the Golden Fleece of Spain, with its red ribbon pendent from his neck; the "Fleece" itself lying upon the blue ribbon of the Garter. The Duke was much too smart a man to wear his "George" upon his thigh. The "George" could only just be perceived above his right hip. The Golden Fleece was believed to be the one that had been worn by the Emperor Charles V.; and to have been given him as a special honour. The Duke wore round his neck a peculiar cravat, not easy to describe. The white cambric was in numerous folds in front, without a bow or tie; and was fastened into a broad buckle, several inches deep, at the back of his neck. His silvery hair was combed forward. I have frequently seen him standing in a ball-room; looking on with a kind smile; evidently pleased at seeing others happy; speaking cordially to those who addressed him ; and certainly, to the last, in the fullest possession of his perceptive faculties. At

E

his own house he played the host well; even at his great age showing a real knowledge of the individual; and a wish to please him or her.

PESTERED as he must have been all his life, with attentions, many of them insincere, he never showed in his manner consciousness of the annoyance.

HIS WAS A FACE that would have been picked out of thousands by anyone who had read of him; and knew his history; and his marvellous exploits.

I never remember to have seen anyone who surpassed him in thoroughly well bred demeanour. With perfect Dignity, his manner was gentle in the extreme. At the same time, I cannot imagine Impertinence itself venturing to take the slightest liberty with him.

During the last few years of his life his look was certainly senile; not that his mind was in any degree affected; but, from being partially deaf, having lost many years before, the use of one ear from the accident of a cannon being discharged close to him, this ailment, no doubt, gave him occasionally a vacant look.

There was one man, and only one man, speaking

the English language, who dared to utter a vile sneer :

" I blot not my page with his name."

With infamous taste, which brought down upon him the contempt of everyone whose opinion was worth having, he quoted publicly, in allusion to the Duke, Johnson's well-known line

" Down Marlborough's cheeks the tears of dotage flow."

This was absolutely false. I know well those who had intimate relations with the Duke to the last: he was as acute at his extreme old age as he had ever been.

The following occurred when Lord Derby's Government was formed in 1852, very shortly before the Duke's death. A list of the new Government was read to him : he being at the time Commander in Chief. Listening carefully, he observed that the Secretary *at* War, in those days a subordinate officer, had been omitted from the list read out. He asked " Who is Secretary at War? " The answer, given with hesitation, was " Beresford "; this being the notorious W. B. a noisy and foolish Irishman. The

Duke, who did not consider such an appointment possible, thought it was his old friend, Marshal Viscount Beresford; and quietly remarked, "A very old man!"

The Duke asked who was Colonial Minister; the Secretary *for* War at that time being also Minister for the Colonies. The reply was "Pakington." "Who?" said the Duke in a loud voice. "Pakington; Sir John Pakington." "Never heard of the gentleman!" said the Duke.

Two incidents that occurred in Sir John's Naval career always charmed me. Sir John paid a visit to one of the Queen's finest ships lying at Spithead. He was accompanied by the Naval Lords of the Admiralty, of which he was then First Lord; and others.

Walking round the Ship in a solemn manner, with the Captain, he overheard a Naval Lord immediately behind him say to the First Lieutenant of the ship "I observe your yards are not so square as they might be." On leaving the Ship, immediately before descending to his boat, while the Marines presented arms, Sir John turned to the Captain, and, after some graceful compliments as to the condition of his ship, added in a stage whisper "There is one thing I observe Captain —— the only thing that I can criticise; and that is that your yards are not perfectly square."

Whether the Captain was astounded by this technical knowledge; or whether he was sharp enough to read Sir John, History does not record.

This, however, was nothing to what followed. It is the custom, it appears, when the Lords of the Admiralty visit a Man-of-War, or are in any boat conveying them in their official capacity, for the First Lord to steer the boat. Admiral Lord Hardwicke, a rough and tough old salt, known in the Navy as 'Old Blowhard,' and the Junior Lords of the Admiralty, were in the boat; which was propelled with great velocity from Spithead to Portsmouth by a number of stalwart oarsmen. All went well while they were in the open sea, which was smooth; but Sir John, whose knowledge of boats was confined to those on a river, steering on the occasion in question, and wishing to do everything "secundum artem," at each stroke of the oars bent forward; as may be seen every day on the Thames. No one interfered with him; and, as I have said, all went well until they approached the landing stairs. The most awful catastrophe then ensued. Sir John, instead of giving the word, or its

Naval equivalent, to "back water," wishing to do the
thing correctly, said "Oars up" or "Oars in." His
ignorance of dynamics at once showed itself. The
prow of the boat struck the piles of the landing stage
with fearful force; and the Lords of the Admiralty,
and half the crew, with Sir John Pakington on the top
of them, were precipitated into the bottom of the
boat. I have been told that Lord Hardwicke's
language was dreadful beyond belief. The pent-up
rage of the fine old seaman, who had been watching
this landsman playing his antics during the day,
fairly boiled over at this hideous disaster. Nothing
in the History of Naval Objurgation had been heard
like his expressions.

NOTHING in the Duke's life shows his lofty sense of
honour more than in relation to his Marriage. Some
years before his return to England from India, he had
engaged himself to a relation, the daughter of Lord
Longford. During his absence the lady had the misfortune, a common one in those days, to catch the
small-pox; and was terribly disfigured by it; so much
so that the Duke did not recognize her when he met
her in Society on his return. The lady with true
nobleness of character, wrote to him telling him that

she considered him under the circumstances of her disfigurement absolutely free from his engagement. Years may possibly have diminished his attachment; and I have never heard that it was exceptionally strong. The Duke, however, felt that in his position, looked up to as he was, as an example of what was right, the fact of his breaking off the marriage, even with the full sanction of his intended wife, would have a very bad effect. Numerous officers in his army were, possibly, similarly, or nearly similarly, placed; and, had he set the example, no doubt in many places engagements of a serious kind would have been broken. He accordingly married the lady; who was a most excellent person in every respect.

THE PHYSICAL exhaustion which the Duke had to endure in Spain would have broken down the health of a man of less strength. For the first three years he never slept out of his clothes; the hardships of his life could hardly have been surpassed.

He always said "The worst house is better than the best tent."

The food in Spain, which even in quiet times is very bad, must have been execrable during his campaign.

The Duke felt that all rested upon him: that he

was the first ; and the rest nowhere ; and that on his
mind, and, to use his own term, his "iron hand"
everything depended. Worried by the 'Juntas' of
Portugal, and Spain ; with the overwhelming responsibility in relation, not only to his army but to theirs ;
surrounded by Jealousy, Envy, and their subordinate,
Malignity, it seems marvellous that any human being
could live ; and preserve his intellect unimpaired.

MANY SUPPOSE that the boot known as the "Wellington" boot was a name. This is quite erroneous.
The Duke himself invented the boot ; and for this
good reason. He found that if, in a campaign, the
surface of the boot of a horse- or foot-soldier became
soaked with moisture, the man could neither pull it
off, nor, as an Irishman would say, pull it on again.
He therefore insisted upon the use of what is known
as the "Wellington" boot. By this means the
external trouser, or, in the Cavalry, the 'over-all,' as it
was called, absorbed the moisture, the boot itself
remaining comparatively dry. The nondescript half-
boot, known to the school-boy of our days as the
"Blucher," had merely a catch name ; invented to
follow the "Wellington."

When I was at Eton there was the strictest sumptuary law against wearing Wellington boots. The result was that every boy possessed a pair : but, not being allowed to keep them at his Tutor's or Dame's house, they were invariably left at the boot-maker's; the first thing done by every boy after he had "got leave" by the mouth of Dr. Hawtrey's butler, Finmore, or

The nameless flunkey with the blue-plushed base,

was to go 'up-town,' and order his Wellington boots to be sent to his rooms. This was "de rigueur;" and I doubt whether any boy at Eton in those days went 'on leave' except in 'Wellingtons.'

HEROIC as was the Duke's endurance of life-long calumny, another, and a very great trait, characterized him. The Nonappreciation, the Misconstruction, the Slander of which he was perpetually the object, not only fell harmless from him : it did not embitter him. Many and many a man, however strong his powers of endurance, must have had the character of his disposition changed by such undeserved, and envenomed animosity; but no amount of injury that was inflicted upon him in this manner changed his noble nature.

His kindness of heart, his extreme benevolence to everyone who sought his assistance, of whatever kind, were not to be surpassed.

SOME OFFICER being mentioned to him as being invariably ' in the thick ' of every fray that took place, and this officer being recommended to him for Command, the Duke quietly said " I prefer to appoint an Officer to an independent command, who keeps out ' of the thick of it ' " : knowing, of course, that an officer could not very well superintend a fight, if he engaged in single combat with one of the enemy.

FOR A MAN so clear-sighted as the Duke, Life could not have offered many enjoyments. Few illusions could have haunted his steady brain : the Chapter of Mankind to all men of acute mental sight is a sad one. Horace Walpole tells us that " Life is a Comedy to those who think ; a Tragedy to those who feel." The Duke probably endeavoured to treat it, more or less, as the former.

To suppose that because he was firm he was hard is the shallowest of blunders. Like Outalissi, in Campbell's beautiful Poem

" As lives the oak unwithered on the rock
By storms above, and barrenness below,
He scorned his own, who felt another's woe."

THE STORY is well known of the Commissary who came to the Duke to complain of the General of his Division. This was attributed to Picton : I have taken the trouble to ascertain that it was of Craufurd of whom the officer spoke. He said to the Duke "General Craufurd, my Lord, says that if the provisions for his Division are not ready in time, he will hang me. What do you advise me to do?" The Duke calmly replied "I strongly advise you to obtain them ; General Craufurd, I observe, keeps his word."

NOTHING REDOUNDED more to the credit of that much abused monarch, George IV., than his consistent, and persistent regard for the Duke of Wellington. I believe that the King's friendship for him was perfectly genuine. The Duke, when out of humour, occasionally sneered at him: but George IV., throughout his whole conduct, from the beginning of the War to his last hour, invariably showed his respect for the

Duke of Wellington. There was no jealousy towards him, as was the case, it is to be feared, between the previous Monarch and Lord Nelson. From the first moment that the Prince Regent got the opportunity of rewarding the Duke, he did so most liberally; and heaped Honours, Titles, and Wealth upon his most deserving subject. He seems to have been never so much pleased as when he was giving the Duke something more: and it is evident that he was proud to have the Duke of Wellington counted among his friends.

George IV. was a man of acute perceptions: it suited the purpose of Byron, and Moore, who ought to have been ashamed of themselves, to write down the King; and to turn him into ridicule: but neither of them pretended that George IV. was a fool. The Duke latterly expressed a high opinion of his intellectual gifts: and indeed it is wonderful, considering the selfish life which George IV. was supposed to have lived as a young man, how he could endure, and retain possession of his senses, the tormenting which he underwent later, in regard to Catholic Emancipation; his Ministers; and other matters. Had he been the self-seeking Sybarite which the Whig Poets and writers represented him to be, he would never have taken the infinite trouble which he did to act a constitutional part, at a terribly difficult crisis in the history of his country.

It was said of George IV. that "he hated without a cause; and never forgave." With strong instincts; and large experience of human nature; he probably read people through; who little dreamed of his powers: and although it may have appeared to the world in general, ignorant of the facts, that he was cynical, and heartless, it is more likely that his alienation was brought about from some secret cause, of which the outside world knew nothing. His conduct to Brummell, whom he had himself selected when a young Hussar at Brighton, appeared to be base: but judging the character of the two men calmly, it seems most probable that Brummell offered the Prince some insult that it was impossible for a man to endure. The Prince Regent, from his position, was absolutely barred from placing himself on a level with anyone who insulted him ; and this, I believe that Brummell, at some time or other, did. It is, of course, known that insanity showed itself in Brummell some years before his death; and, superior in his way, as Brummell undoubtedly was, I suspect that his head was turned by the position which he attained; and that on some occasion he must have offered to his Sovereign some very gross, and unpardonable insult.

No one can form an idea of the peculiar position held by Monarchs. Absolutely isolated by their situation; in some cases not having mixed, even in youth, with their subjects; utterly shut out from the world by a small circle; and totally dependent on that circle for information; great allowances should be made for what may appear fickleness or injustice. George IV. as a young man mixed, of course, much in Society; in fact was much more a part of Society than those who had gone before him. He was therefore, with natural shrewdness, better able to judge, than most of those in his position, of human character. His friendship with the Duke remained unchanged. Nothing can be easier for those who have the ear of a Monarch than with "whispering tongue to poison truth"; and to create a prejudice, the more lasting from its object having no means of defending himself. No doubt George IV.'s Court was made up, in some degree, of unscrupulous men: but I believe that, with the exception of Brummell, there was never any conspicuous case of desertion.

As regards Sheridan, great injustice was done. It was supposed that George IV., having amused himself with Sheridan so long as the latter was amusing, turned his back on him, when Poverty, and Misfortune visited his sick bed. Nothing could be more untrue. Public recognition of Sheridan on the part of the King would hardly have been seemly. Sums of money advanced to the splendid Wit for the purpose of Parliamentary Elections had, I fear there is little doubt, been spent by him in other ways; that money was liberally and secretly sent to him by the King is now well known.

It surprizes me that no one has investigated, nor endeavoured to investigate the question as to what were the personal opinions of Monarchs in history. We know that generation after generation has lavished Criticism, frequently Contempt, and occasionally Vituperation upon those who have occupied thrones : but we have had no opportunity of knowing what the Monarch himself thought of his contemporaries. Entirely unable from their position to reply to Criticism, or Abuse; compelled to sit still while every sort of interpretation is being put upon their acts by those vile minds which invent, where they cannot find, vileness; one would like to hear the " Case of the King," as stated by himself. Many Monarchs have been persons of exceptional ability; well able to defend themselves if they had the opportunity: but History does not record one case of the defence of a King by himself. A few casual observations have been handed down; and that is all.

How much one would like to know, for instance, George IV.'s private opinion of his slanderers. He found Moore good company; and he admired Byron. He never lost an opportunity of showing kindness, and doing what was good-natured, by both. Byron and Moore turned upon him mercilessly. We have never heard the disagreeable things that George IV. might have said about them; possibly a good many.

The gossips of each age would be delighted if George IV. had told us the original, deep-seated reason for his inextinguishable hatred of his wife.

One would have liked to have heard the opinions of George III.; who had to do, in his day, with a great many conspicuous persons; what he thought of Lord Bute in his boyhood; whether he really liked William Pitt. One would like to have heard his grandfather's opinion of Sir Robert Walpole, the dominant spirit of England for so many years. Queen Anne's views, clearly expressed, in relation to her brother; and to the Protestant Succession; would be interesting.

What would not Charles II.'s witty account of Lord Clarendon be worth?

Of James I. and his friends, the less said the better.

How gratifying it would be to know from Queen Elizabeth which, on the whole, she preferred; the handsome, and chivalrous Essex, or the broad-shouldered, and brutal Leicester: and whether she had such another satisfactory moment in her life as that in which she endeavoured to shake the remains of life out of old Lady Nottingham.

Edward VI. kept a diary; and we find the item "The Lord Protector beheaded this morning." The young King, however, was discreet; and wrote his memoranda in Greek characters. He cannot be expected to have expressed what he felt, or what we hope he felt, on the occasion of his kind uncle's death.

How interesting would be Henry VIII.'s real views as regards the Reformation; and his position in relation to Sir Thomas More; whether Sir Thomas More privately expressed to King Henry the opinion that he would make an excellent head of a Christian Church; and whether the condemning Sir Thomas

More to the fate to which he had himself condemned others made any difference in the personal relations between the great Chancellor and his King. Probably King Henry could have told queer stories about Cardinal Wolsey.

Shakespeare has given us Queen Margaret's views with regard to the Wars of the Roses; but her memoranda, written by herself, would have been very interesting.

I should like to have asked Edward I. whether he had anything to say for himself in reference to the foully barbarous execution of Sir Simon Fraser, on Tower Hill.

To go further back: Julius Cæsar gave us his Commentaries; but has not told us what he personally thought of Brutus, and the Senators: whether he believed them to be friends; or always suspected them to be traitors, who would sooner or later destroy him. We should like to have heard his impartial opinion as regards Cleopatra; and from the last-named Monarch to have heard her comparisons between Augustus, and Antony. She might have told us whether in her heart she despised the latter for giving up a world for her sake; and whether she did not in reality prefer a man who did not care for her.

We should like to have heard from Augustus why he banished Ovid; a secret that has been completely kept from mankind.

In short, there is no limit to the questions which we should like to put to the Monarchs of the past.

NAPOLEON took a conventional, and a vulgar view of the British race. His utter want of just appreciation brought about his ruin. He judged men according to commonplace rules. He met with a people that was not commonplace;

"With daring aims; Irregularly Great":

and they annihilated him.

He believed that in the field, as in politics, once he had established a commanding position, his enemy would yield. He found out his mistake.

Napoleon III. was far wiser: he had lived among us; and understood us; and although, as a last card, I have no doubt whatever that he would have attacked us, it would have been his very last card; and would have been played with great apprehensions for his own safety.

I HEARD from the 2nd Duke particulars of Lord Castlereagh's end. He had heard a good deal about it from his father. The Duke observed Lord Castlereagh's behaviour at the Cabinet Council; and, leaving it, he went straight to Dr Bankhead, the first Physician of that day. Not finding him at home, the Duke returned again; rode to the Park; and, on his way home, the Physician still being absent, wrote on his visiting card, which I believe still exists, " Either Lord L. is mad or I am.—W." Lord Castlereagh had become, by his father's death, Marquess of Londonderry, in the Peerage of Ireland. The rest is known : even the active treatment which Dr Bankhead used was not sufficient to save the unfortunate man's life. The Duke told me that his father was absolutely certain that Lord Castlereagh had been mad for some time; worn out by work: and that the horrible conspiracy, which his imagination pictured, was a sheer hallucination. No trace of it whatever could be found after his death.

AN ATTEMPT was made on Sir Robert Peel's life, which has never been made public. His second daughter, one of the most beautiful, and amiable women that I have known, told me, that on one public, or semi-public occasion, her father and mother were going through the City in a closed carriage.

Lady Peel sat on the right. The door on the right was opened; and a man presented a pistol. Seeing that Lady Peel was in the place in which he expected to find Sir Robert, he withdrew his arm; closed the door; and disappeared. She added that this occurrence, which she had from her father, and mother, had never been made known. She was unable to recollect the precise occasion.

THE DUKE, when a young man, lost a sum, important for him, at play; he discouraged gambling among officers.

Crockford's was an Institution that, I regret to say, I never saw. The splendid palace, still existing, on the West side of St James's Street, was not, as is supposed, the actual scene of Play. These grand rooms, magnificently furnished in the style of the Renaissance, were used for ordinary club purposes. The gambling room was in the small house, which adjoins the building on the South. The reason of this was that, in case an indictment had been brought, the actual Club itself would not have been sacrificed. For those who chose to ruin themselves, Crockford's was no doubt a bad place; but for the more sensible portion of the Club, who were

content to lose a few hundreds for the good of the
House, it must have been charming. To find the
best society in the world under circumstances of
excitement, must have been truly delightful.

The following incident occurred at the end of
Crockford's career : I have thought it worthy of
being put into verse :

A CHRONICLE OF CROCKFORD'S.

The Derby is lost, and the Derby is won ;
The race of all Races has come and is gone ;
So homeward each whirls, whether loser and sad,
Or winner of "flimsies" with countenance glad :

When in ROME a grand Triumph enlivened the Road,
That leads to the Victor's Imperial abode,
"Via Sacra" they called it; so multitudes greet
The Winners who climb up St James' holy Street.

"Thou art mortal!" still whispers a voice in each ear :
Some have paid for life's whistle uncommonly dear ;
As at CROCKFORD's they glance, 'twixt a sigh and a
     frown,
Some remember won money's not always one's own.

On the eve of the DERBY a whisper had spread;
A ridiculous rumour that " CROCKY" was dead;
A tale that had faded ere brightened the looks
Of the " Jeunesse dorée " who were deep in his books.

There he sits, in a window, as four-year-old fresh;
Rather paler than usual, but still in the flesh;
With NUGEE's best surtout; and a faultless cravat:
Some old friends he salutes; to some touches his hat.

No choice but to pay; all the winners are known:
To the usurer's dovecot the " flimsies " have flown:
And the payers ne'er knew, till a twelvemonth had
  sped,
That the man in the window was " CROCKY," but—
  dead.

ONE CHARACTER in the great European drama
of the beginning of the century has become faint: the
Archduke Charles of Austria. The Duke of Wellington, and Napoleon, had a very high opinion of
him. In one place the Duke says that the Archduke
excelled them both. My uncles, Sir Charles, and
General Robert Craufurd, served under him. The
former was desperately wounded on the Rhine.

The Archduke Charles had one extraordinary peculiarity; not in the least the result of intemperance : up to five o'clock in the afternoon his intellect was splendid; but, for some mysterious cause, it faded out at that hour.

NAPOLEON I., though he must have faced death often in the battle-field, could never summon sufficient resolution to swallow a black dose ; a most horrible trial, as everyone must admit, to a generation that had to take them : but it seems singular that he had not philosophy enough to go through this abominable and, as it now seems, unnecessary horror.

IT WAS SAID in 1815, as to the letter repeated over and over again on public buildings, " Nous avons les ' N ' mis partout."

Some one speaking of the empty chariot brought to Paris from S⁺ Mark's, Venice, asked who was to stand in it. The answer was "The Emperor." "Ah ! le char l'attend." A good story murdered by Sir Walter Scott.

Said of Charles X. in 1830, " L'ex, et lent Roi " is not a bad pun.

THE DUKE FIGURED conspicuously at the Coronation of Her present Majesty: Canon Barham of
St Paul's mentions him in "Mr. Barney Maguire's"
ballad on the subject in the "Ingoldsby Legends," as

> " Wellington walking
> With his swoord drawn, talking
> To Hill, and Hardinge, haroes of great fame."

Some of the phrases in this Poem are now obscure:
it will save future generations trouble if I clear them
up: "The Prince of Potboys" is a delicate allusion
to Prince Putbus, the Ambassador of the King of
Prussia.

> " 'Twould have made you crazy
> To see Esterhazy
> All jools from his jasey to his di'mond boots."

I remember Lord D., now Lord D. and A., who
knew Barham well, telling me at Christ Church that
'Jasey' was a word invented for the rhyme; and had
no meaning: I suggested that it was a cant name for
a wig: I have heard since that it is an ecclesiastical
ornament, worn on the breast.

Of another passage I have been asked the interpretation ;

> " Och ! the Count von Strogonoff,
> Sure he got prog enough,
> The sly ould divil undernathe the stairs."

The meaning is as follows : Boards were placed horizontally behind and above the Peers' and Peeresses' seats raised in a high slope in the North and South Transepts : on these privileged persons were seated : there were, however, no boards placed vertically, except here and there for support : the result being that those who put their cocked hats, swords, sandwiches, etc., under their seats, lost them : the articles falling in an intermittent cascade to the floor of the Abbey below. Luncheons innumerable disappeared ; and the incident immortalized by the Poet may no doubt have occurred ; the individual being selected, I suspect as a brother Poet, for the sake of the rhyme.

There were fearful articles called "portable dinners" invented for the occasion ; which, were said to contain in one lozenge so much nourishment as a leg of mutton : they drove those who were so imprudent as to eat them, almost mad from thirst.

THE DUKE was strongly in favour of preserving the

army-rank of Lieutenant-Colonel for Captains in the Guards. When asked his reason he replied: "In case of another war I must have young officers, about whom I know something, to command the Second Battalions which will be raised."

THE DUKE was naturally impatient of the endless portraits that were insisted upon. He exclaimed one day, "They have painted me in every attitude, except standing on my head."

The numerous portraits of the Duke in the character sketches by H. B. give some idea of him ; but not one that I have been able to find exactly represents him.

THE EXPRESSION has been used, with a half sneer, in relation to the Duke, of his excellent "Common Sense." This much abused term is supposed by many to represent a common, or ordinary quality ; the fact being that "Common Sense" means the collective Wisdom of generations ; which is occasionally found concentrated in the mind of one individual ; as it was in his. The envious majority of Mankind will not admit the word "Wisdom" to be applied to any human being ; and they basely attribute to the term

"Common Sense" the meaning "which is common":
thereby hoping to disparage the glorious quality,
which ought to bear another name.

IT HAS BEEN said that Genius is an "infinite capacity for taking pains." This seems to me to be an
error. That it is a quality which Genius possesses;
and without which Genius cannot succeed, I have no
doubt. The Duke had it as regards War and Diplomacy in the highest degree.

He said "If you want a thing done well, do it yourself."

THE ARMIES of great nations have been created by
individuals. This was the case with the conquering
armies of Pompey, and of Cæsar : and, in later days,
Europe has produced the same results.

The Prussian Army was created by Frederick II. ;
the French Army was created by Napoleon ; and the
British Army owed its existence to the Duke of
Wellington. In each case a master mind had to deal
with the materials : and in each case the results were
brilliant.

ONE OF THE MOST striking scenes in the dra-
matic life of the Duke was that in the Theatre of

the University of Oxford, when he was inaugurated as Chancellor. A spectator, who now worthily represents the University in Parliament, has described the scene to me. The Duke, sitting in his splendid robes of black and gold as Chancellor: everyone who was distinguished in the University about him: encompassed by the great men who had, in some degree, shared his glorious career; the English Prize-Poem was recited. On the occasion every element was present that could impress the hearers. The subject of the Poem was "The Hospice of St Bernard"; its author Joseph Arnould, of Wadham College. I have the Poem, not easy to obtain, before me now. It is of some length. There is naturally an allusion to the passage of Mount St Bernard, equivocally related of Hannibal, and Charlemagne; really of their rival, the 1st Napoleon. The latter is not dwelt on to any extent.

The great effect produced was, as is almost essential, by a surprize.

The Poet, standing in the rostrum, turned slightly to the left, in the direction of the Chancellor; and gave these lines with marked emphasis:

" When on that field, where last the Eagle soared,
War's mightier Master wielded Britain's sword:

And the dark soul a World could scarce subdue
Bent to thy Genius, Chief of Waterloo !"

bowing at the same time to the Duke.   My informant
tells me that never could he have conceived a scene
of such wild enthusiasm as that which ensued.

The Undergraduates in the galleries rose to their
feet, and for five minutes continued cheering; joined,
of course, by the Masters on the floor of the Theatre :
the ladies who were present waving their handker-
chiefs.   There was then a pause : and the Poet
endeavoured to go on ; but he was again and again
interrupted by vociferous cheering ; in fact it seemed
as if the noise would never come to an end.

During the whole of this scene the Duke sat like a
Statue ; apparently unmoved : after a time motioning
to the Poet to continue.

The Poem may be found in "Oxford Prize
Poems; 1839."   The copy which I have is of
remarkable value in consequence of its containing
a Poem by John Ruskin of Ch. Ch. called " Salsette
and Elephanta," recited in 1839.   It contains Poems
by some who have since played a more or less conspicuous part in their generation : one, a Congratulatory Address recited by E. Cardwell of Baliol ; and

one recited, but not written, by Lord Maidstone,
afterwards Lord Winchilsea; author of "A Paraphrase
of the Book of Job"; and "The Tommiad." The
latter was under the impression that the lines above
quoted, relating to the Duke, were part of those
recited by him, but this was not so. It does not
state in the volume by whom the lines recited by
Lord Maidstone were written; but I have ascertained
that they were by Dr Bull, whom I remember as a
portly Canon of Ch. Ch. No matter by whom: they
are worthless. There is a Poem in the volume on
"The Burning of Moscow," by W. L. Seymour Fitz-
gerald, of Oriel, 1835; another by Frederic Faber, of
University College, on the "Knights of St John,"
1836; and one on "The Gipsies," by Arthur Penrhyn
Stanley, of Baliol, 1837. Of an earlier race, the
volume has "Palestine," by Reginald Heber, of
Brazenose, 1803: and, best of all, "The Belvidere
Apollo," by Henry Hart Milman, of the same College,
1812.

A STORY was told of General Grant, the great
American President and warrior, which fascinated me.
General Grant was invited to dine at Apsley House
by the 2nd Duke of Wellington. A most distinguished

party assembled to meet him. During a pause, in the middle of dinner, the ex-President, addressing the Duke at the head of the table, said "My Lord, I have heard that your father was a military man. Was that the case?"

I HAVE DESCRIBED the review given to the Emperor Nicholas when at Windsor in 1844. An incident occurred during his stay at the Castle that is worth recording. A boy told me that he had been for a walk, "after four," on the North terrace of the Castle. On this terrace are the windows of the low rooms on the ground floor, at one time occupied by my friend, and brother officer Sir Thomas Biddulph, an important member of the Queen's Household; and and at an earlier period by the unfortunate Monarch, George III. while insane; I assume because they were quiet; more or less secluded from the rest of the Castle; and easily accessible. There is a small ledge or ramp, which would enable anyone, as it enabled me after hearing the story, to look into these rooms. The boy told me that, walking along the terrace, he heard the sound of voices, and from natural curiosity he climbed on to this ledge; and looked in at the window. He distinctly saw Sir Robert Peel sitting

near the fireplace ; the Emperor Nicholas walking up
and down the room ; speaking very loudly, and
gesticulating. This was narrated to me within an
hour of the fact having occurred. It will be remembered that in his conversations with Sir Hamilton
Seymour, which were published, and which Sir
Hamilton Seymour subsequently repeated to me, the
Emperor Nicholas said that, when in England, he
had conversed with three important members of the
Queen's Government. They were, no doubt, Sir
Robert Peel, the Duke of Wellington, and Lord
Aberdeen. The Emperor said that one only of the
three personages in question had agreed with him
with regard to his projects in the East, in which he
wished the British Government to take part. The
other two sternly refused to entertain his proposals.
I have no doubt that this conversation, half overheard
by the Eton boy, was on the subject which brought
such misfortunes upon that part of the world ; and
such slaughter upon three great races.

THE FOLLOWING STORY has been told ; but
I have not met with it in its absolute correctness.
The Duke of Wellington received a letter when sitting
in the House of Lords, from the eminent landscape

designer, and great authority on botanical matters, J. C. Loudon. The Duke had lost sight of him for some years. It was a note to this effect: "My lord Duke : It would gratify me extremely if you would permit me to visit Strathfieldsaye, at any time convenient to your Grace, and to inspect the 'Waterloo beeches.' Your Grace's faithful servant, J. C. Loudon." The Waterloo beeches were trees that had been planted immediately after the battle of Waterloo; as a memorial of the great fight. The Duke read the letter twice, the writing of which was not very clear; and, with his usual promptness and politeness, replied as follows; having read the signature as "C. J. London," instead of "J. C. Loudon ":

"My dear Bishop of London

"It will always give me great pleasure to see you at Strathfieldsaye. Pray come there whenever it suits your convenience; whether I am at home or not.

"My servant will receive orders to show you so many pairs of breeches of mine as you wish; but why you should wish to inspect those that I wore at the battle of Waterloo is quite beyond the comprehension of

"Yours most truly

"WELLINGTON."

This letter was received, as may be supposed, with great surprize by the Bishop of London. He showed it to the Archbishop of Canterbury, and to other discreet persons: they came to the melancholy conclusion that the great Duke of Wellington had evidently lost his senses.

The Bishop of London (Blomfield) declared that he had not written to the Duke for two years; and to receive this extraordinary intimation puzzled the whole Bench of Bishops.

Explanations, however, of a satisfactory kind, followed: and the friendship of these worthy men was not changed.

I HAVE USED colloquial titles, as it would seem absurd, and certainly contrary to the "manner of speaking," to say 'the Marquess of this did that;' or the 'Earl of that said this.' As regards an individual Peer, the approximate date in Sir Bernard Burke's edition of the 'British Bible' will indicate which of his race he was.

I KNEW the man, whom the Duke of Wellington selected as a tutor for his sons, well. He was the Vicar of Brighton. His name was Wagner; the

father of a clergyman who became subsequently a
very conspicuous member of the Ritualist party.
His character was not unlike that of the Duke : firm,
determined, calm, positive in his views, and acting
up to them. At one time there were symptoms of
Parochial mutiny at Brighton. Wagner would stand
no nonsense : and ultimately triumphed over the
attempts which had been made against his authority.

THE TERM, now become a part of the language
" Circumstances over which I have no controul"
originated with the Duke of Wellington.

SOON AFTER HIS FIRST BATTLE, the great
Victory of Assaye, in which, with three thousand
British, and some black troops, the Duke routed
over thirty thousand Maharattas, the best troops in
India, he was taken to visit a female Magician famous
throughout Hindostan. This person presented him
with a sword, traditionally believed to have belonged
to Genghiz Khan, the Conqueror of India. The Pro-
phetess told him, at the same time, that he would be
the greatest Conqueror in the World.

This sword the Duke wore in all his battles. It
was lost for some years. The sword was ultimately

recognized at an Auction Room, at the sale of Sir Thomas Lawrence's effects. It was bought for thirty shillings; and given back to the Duke; who was delighted at its recovery.

WELLINGTON.

Before the dark Enchantress
  The firm-faced Victor stands ;
Her cavern in the desert rock
  'Mid India's burning sands :

" Wear this; a mighty Conqueror's Sword,
  Ay, gird it on thy thigh ;
And wave it where it has been waved,
  In the van of Victory !

" That Sabre through long years has hung ;
  For never yet my soul
Has felt the presence of the Man
  Red blazoned in Fate's scroll.

" Go ! Man of Men ! in Battle's storm
  Raise o'er thy head the brand !
Through waves of blood, on War's proud mane
  Place fearlessly thy hand !

" In visions on my soul that crowd
　　I see thy Banners fly,
Where Thunders rive the battlement,
　　And hide in storm the sky :

" I see thy baffled foes return,
　　Where Havoc strews their path ;
Where Murder and foul Rapine stalk,
　　And all is Fire and Death.

" Then, borne on Valour's pinions, sweep
　　Thy Armies to pursue ;
Thy Lion-race shall crown their Chief
　　Where the plume-stripped Eagle flew.

" Fame's dazzling honours deck thy breast ;
　　A world's Renown is thine :
When thy country greets thy Glory, think
　　What Prophecy was mine !

" But brighter yet a vision glows,
　　Ay ! nobler yet thy Fame ;
A terror-stricken world shall call
　　Upon thy saving name :

"The Nations cast on thee their **Hope** ;
  Their Power at thy feet ;
That Sword shall deck thee on the day,
  When warring Empires meet :

" Thy Comrades who around thee fight
  Shall fall among the slain ;
But thou shalt bear a charmèd **life**
  Upon that Northern plain.

" When through that day, that long, dark day,
  The lurid clouds have spread,
A Sunburst at the evening hour
  Shall blaze above thy head :

" Then, Soldier ! is thy Triumph's hour,
  The hour that's sealed by Fate :
Go, Hero ! Of the Sons of Men
  Most fitly called ' The Great.' "

                                W. F.

THE DUKE, at Waterloo, was Colonel of the Blues :
and, before a charge, said " Now, Gentlemen, for the
honour of the Household Troops."

On that day, when the Household Cavalry Brigade
under Lord Edward Somerset was returning from a

successful advance, the Duke raised his cocked hat;
and said "Life Guards! I thank you." I have these
words from one who was present.

THE DUKE was a frequent visitor when in Paris,
during the occupation, of the celebrated Madame
Craufurd; it was on his return from an evening party
at her house that he was fired at; this lady was the
wife of my great grand-uncle. Mr Quentin Craufurd,
her husband, was the younger brother of my great
grandfather, Sir Alexander Craufurd; and an Indian
Nabob. He bequeathed the whole of his vast fortune, not to his relations, but to the grand-daughter
of Madame Craufurd, the beautiful Duchess de Gram-
mont, sister of Alfred Count d'Orsay.

Madame Craufurd was for many years one of the
principal ladies of fashion in Paris: her salon being
in the Rue d'Anjou.

THE DUKE was asked by a lady if the innumerable
Caricatures which had been published of him in the
course of his life had ever caused him annoyance.
He answered "Not a bit! not a bit!" and then;
after a pause; "There's only one Caricature that
has ever caused me annoyance: Douro."

THE FRIEND and confidante of Byron, Wellington, and Disraeli; in constant correspondence with Emperors and Kings; with intellect to appreciate the various changes that took place in her long life in European affairs, the volume of Sarah Lady Jersey's life would have been priceless. "I was the one thing he loved," said she, in my hearing, after the Duke's death. I believe that at one time the Duke had great admiration for her half-sister, Lady Georgiana Fane, who did not marry; and that during the Waterloo campaign he took a kind interest in several young ladies; and addressed to them letters in the same terms as have lately been published. Of course these attachments were purely Pickwickian. The Duke was an Augustus, not an Antony; and I do not suppose that he at any time was ever influenced in his actions by female power.

The state of London society during Lady Jersey's career can hardly be imagined now. Within the last few years all evening entertainments on a large scale have ceased. No large houses are open: in fact the London season, which was supposed to be dying, is now, in this respect, absolutely defunct: an earlier change came over London society, as I have heard it described, at the time of the Reform Bill of 1832.

The effect of Politics upon Society manifested itself
very soon. The most exclusive assembly in the world
was, as is well known, Almack's. I have heard that
the original Almack came from the Highlands; that
his real name was MacCall, and that it was to avoid
the odium which, in the middle of the last century,
attached to Scotchmen that he ingeniously changed his
name to Almack. I believe that the relation to the
rooms of Neil Gow, the great fiddler, who said that no
man could play with effect till he cried at his own playing, thus began. Certain great ladies, of whom Lady
Jersey was one of the principal, were the Patronesses
of these balls; and no one could receive an invitation
except by application to them. The seven battalions
that form the brigade of Guards; and here I trust that
no reader will commit the social shibboleth of even
thinking of any troops but the Foot Guards when the
term "Guards" is used; have about 150 officers: the
reader will be surprized to learn that of this number,
many of them young and dancing men, not more
than fifteen were invited in any one year. This is the
legend: and, I believe, it is founded on truth. The
Duke of Wellington has been blamed by shallow people
for placing his name on the Patronesses' list. The Duke
had the good sense, wishing to attend the balls, to do

as other men did; and to take his chance with them.

THE BEARSKINS of the Officers of the Guards are usually kept in boxes, which can be opened at both ends, in order to preserve their "raven down of darkness." The Duke, however, for some good reason, invariably removed his bearskin from the box in which it was put aside with his own hands: and preferring the appearance of the head-dress when so treated, pulled it out so as to make

" Each particular hair to stand on end."

I CAN CONCEIVE nothing more exhilarating than to have had the opportunity of breathing the air of good sense which surrounded the Duke.

To listen to his clearly and tersely expressed opinions on various subjects must have been refreshing in the highest degree : and those are much to be envied who had these opportunities.

I HAVE READ an interesting letter written by the Right Hon. William Windham, to General Robert Craufurd when in Spain ; in which the Minister expressess his regret that the 30,000 men about to be sent on the unfortunate expedition to Walcheren, should not be landed in the Peninsula.

Toward the end he says: "I begin to think that your chief (the Duke), is really possessed of military talent; and I am sorry that the troops will not be placed under his command in the Peninsula. Depend upon it no expedition can succeed, however well organized, that is placed under the command of such a man as the Earl of Chatham."

This prophecy was too sadly fulfilled.

THE DUKE'S POLITICAL CAREER is an answer to those shallow persons who declare that in Politics nothing is required beyond good sense.

To do anything well requires good sense; whether to paint a picture; or to amputate a limb: and any-one attempting to do either of these things, unless they have good sense will inevitably fail; but the most sensible reader, unless he be a specialist, would hesitate to paint a picture, or even to amputate a leg. In the former case he would only bring ridicule upon himself; in the last he would inevitably cause the death of the patient.

The government of a country such as ours, with its political system more complicated than that of any nation that ever existed, is hardly to be taken up in middle life; or carried on successfully by men possessing no quality except good sense.

There is a passage in "Prince Albert's Golden Precepts," 1862, in which the Prince Consort says: "Nobody will tell me that Genius would not take an incomparably higher flight, if supplied with the means which knowledge can impart : or that Common Sense does not become only truly powerful, when in possession of the materials upon which Judgment is to be exercised." Applied Good Sense will do wonders : Good Sense without special knowledge and application will not govern States. This, however, is a notion which is evidently fast dying out.

Having been an observer for many years of the House of Commons ; its ways, and the best method for its treatment, I should say that to influence it requires a man of exceptional intellect, unlimited energy, unwearied perseverance ; and, above all, for him to have made it the specialty of his life.

The Duke passed the best years of his life elsewhere : and, though early holding office as Secretary for Ireland, a good seven years had been passed by him away from his country.

That he did his best no one can doubt : that his best was a failure few will hesitate to say.

THE COMMON IDEA that Napoleon called us a "Nation of Shopkeepers" is a delusion. The Phrase was never used as quoted : the term "Nation boutiquière" was used, not by Napoleon, but by Barrère in a speech made in the National Assembly on the subject of Lord Howe's victory of the 1ˢᵗ June. The speech was delivered on 28 Prairial; Monday, June 16; 1794. The passage is this; "Let Pitt then boast of this victory to his 'Nation boutiquière.' Already do the English newspapers announce that a division of our fleet has taken a Dutch convoy. But we can tell you better news. Not a day passes but the commerce of our enemies affords us provisions of wealth. Here then is what the French Marine has done; now that it is rid of its vermin Nobility."

The speech is to be found in "The Register of the Times"; published 1794; page 72. Some pages earlier, page 9, another delusion is dispelled. The following, signed by Lord Howe, is the "List of French Ships captured on the 1ˢᵗ day of June, 1794:

'La Juste,'	80 guns ;
'Sans Pareil,'	80 „
'L'America,'	74 „
'L'Achille,'	74 „
'Northumberland,'	74 „
'L'Impétueux,'	74 „
'Vengeur,'	74 „ : sunk al-

most immediately upon being taken possession of" ;
not with her flag flying.

THE 2ND DUKE was, I should say, not unlike what
his father had been in middle life : a thin, hollow face,
the configuration of the head of the same sort; but
smaller than his father's; a very pleasant, and kind
smile ; having rather the manner of an 'enfant gaté ';
who, being born to everything that the world can give,
did not derive much enjoyment from the gift.

As a rule, good-natured ; and willing to go out of
his way, and to take a little trouble to do anyone a
kindness ; an acute observer, and a good reader of .
character. He once wrote to me that he had never
presumed to wear his father's sword.

Immediately on inheriting Apsley House he removed the boards which had been placed on the
front railings, to prevent a crowd assembling to see

the 1ˢᵗ Duke mount and dismount from his horse : saying at the time " I don't think a crowd is ever likely to assemble to see me get on to my horse."

He had a good seat himself on horseback ; and was by no means unlike his father when mounted, at a certain distance.

He once or twice said that I ought to come to Apsley House ; and make a catalogue raisonnée of the various objects that had belonged to his father. Wishing, of course, not to intrude, I did not remind him of this suggestion. I regret it now : although pains have evidently been taken, in showing the objects of great interest that are displayed there.

The Duke told me that the amount of manuscript found after his father's death was beyond all belief.

AS REGARDS the historical exclamation of the Duke, " Up Guards ; and at them ! " it is too theatrical ; and not like him. My own belief is that, .having given the general order to advance, through his Staff Officers, he rode along the flank of the Battalions of Guards, who were lying down by order : the Duke probably used a well-known phrase, " Now Guards : up and at 'em ; up and at 'em ! " just as a school-boy would say " Up and at him ! "

The Duke himself said he could not remember whether he had said it, or not.

THE DUKE was asked whether he cared much about an exceptionally good dinner; his questioner added that Lord Douro was particularly fond of what was nice. The Duke replied: "I like a good dinner when it is set before me: Douro will take the trouble to order one." A large section of the discriminating portion of Mankind will answer as the Duke.

A LADY said to the Duke "I suppose, Duke, during your life you have inspired a great deal of admiration, and enthusiasm among women, both abroad and at home." The Duke at once replied "Oh, yes, plenty of that! plenty of that! but no woman ever loved me: never in my whole life."

IT IS KNOWN that the Duke, being asked to present the sum bequeathed to the bravest man in the British Army, refusing it himself, selected General Sir James Macdonnell, who divided the money with Sergeant Graham, of the Coldstream Guards, who assisted him in closing the door at the rear of

H

Hougomont. This shut out a party of Frenchmen; who had crept round under the western wall. I knew Sir James Macdonnell well. He carried his recklessness, as regards fire, into old age. On one occasion I was shooting with a large party in Berkshire. The coppice was very dense; it was difficult to see a few yards in front. We noticed, however, that every now and then a gun was fired immediately in front of the line; apparently about fifteen yards. A gentleman who was shooting on my right said "Who can that be in front?" I went forward and discovered Sir James Macdonnell. He appeared totally regardless of the circumstance that at any moment a charge of shot might be lodged in the small, or rather the large, of his back. I remonstrated with him; but I have forgotten whether he changed his position. However, he was not shot.

THE DEPUTY QUARTER-MASTER GENERAL, who was in attendance on the Duke's person at Waterloo was one of his favourite officers; and I believe that the Duke felt his death more than that of anyone else. Sir William de Lancy resembled the Duke in face; and the idea obtained at one time that the French deliberately fired at him ; under the impression that he was the Duke of Wellington. He was close to the Duke when killed.

The Duke, in after life, said that he could not remember whether he wore a cloak at Waterloo or not. He wore one in the early part of the day : in the afternoon, when the weather became warmer, he took it off. Sir William de Lancy, for the Duke's convenience, was fastening the Duke's cloak on to the front of his, Sir William's, saddle ; he being dismounted. At this moment he was struck fatally. Believing that he would die in a few minutes, he urged his attendants to leave him, and join the battle. This heroic action, it is to be feared, cost him his life. He was found the next morning alive ; and lived for some days longer in Brussels. Possibly had his wound been attended to at the moment, his valuable life might have been spared. A sharp frost on the night of the 18th saved many lives. Sir William de Lancy was buried in the old cemetery at Brussels, where I saw his grave last year; his body has lately been transferred to the new one. .

THE DUKE said that he was slandered from a boy. Horace Walpole tells us that Calumny usually selects some innocent action ; and places upon it its own false, and foul interpretation. The more honourable and straightforward was the Duke's career, the less would he be appreciated by his miserable slanderers. The Duke felt that his shoulders were broad enough ; and he disregarded his enemies, and their lies, as being ephemeral. As he said in one place " I have acted according to the best of my judgment ; and what the enemy says of me, and what they say of me at home, I do not care." This was the summing up of his great mind.

I VISITED APSLEY HOUSE on the 20th of March 1889, by the kind permission of the Duke of Wellington ; and made a careful and minute inspection of all that had belonged to the great Duke. His Orders, Bâtons, Swords, complimentary plate, and splendid sets of dinner and dessert services are admirably arranged in a room on the ground floor. The late Duke some years ago showed them to me. They were not then in the perfect order in which they now are. Among the Orders there is one that is exceptionally noticeable. The ordinary military Cross of the Bath is of white enamel. After Waterloo the King granted to the Duke of Wellington and to **Lord** Anglesey **to add to** the top of the cross a Royal **Crown.**

THE COLOSSAL STATUE OF NAPOLEON by Canova, holding a small Globe in his right hand surmounted by a statue of Victory, is no doubt placed in its present position, the inner hall, because there was nowhere else to put it: its proportions dwarf the house.

The Duke when he purchased the statue, of Canova, made the obvious remark that the Globe was much too small for the figure. Canova, with Italian adroitness, replied "Your Grace forgets that Great Britain is not included." (La grande Bretagne n'y est pas comprise.)

Pompey's Statue at Rome gives a far finer idea: he holds the Globe in his left hand; as with disregard.

In one room on the 1st floor is a portrait of Mr. Perceval, the Prime Minister, painfully like Robespierre. In the same room is the well known picture by Wilkie of the "Chelsea Pensioners receiving the news of Waterloo." When this picture was first produced, someone, sharper than the average, at once detected a fault; a serious anachronism. The intelligent reader, to whom no doubt the print is familiar,

may exercise his or her ingenuity in finding out
what this is. Opposite to the Wilkie is, I think, the
only poor work that Sir Edwin Landseer ever executed.
It is of Van Amburgh in a Cage of Lions : it is faulty
in almost every respect. The Lions have retained
none of their dignity : and as for Van Amburgh, he
looks as if he were stuffed with sawdust.

In the Ball Room, bringing pleasant recollections,
are some of the best pictures. At the Eastern end is
a fine portrait of Charles I. by Vandyke ; at the
opposite end an indifferent copy of a picture from
Correggio. Over the central mantelpiece is a beautifully soft sketch by Murillo of Isaac blessing either
Esau or Jacob. Apropos of this picture, I appealed
to my friend, an Ex-Lord Chancellor, who accompanied me, as to whether the bequeathment could
not have been set aside. He replied " Certainly."

Looking at the beautiful Titian, of Venus, which is
in this room, I quoted Lord Byron's well known
couplet

> " I've seen much finer women ripe and real
> Than all the nonsense of their stone ideal."

The Ex-Chancellor said " Do you know of whom
Lord Byron wrote that ? " I replied in the negative.

He said "He wrote that of Lady Charlemont."
Lady Charlemont I knew well. She was by birth a
Birmingham, a descendant of a very ancient family,
the Lords Athenry. She was for many years a Lady
in Waiting to the Queen; and certainly in old age
had traces of extraordinary beauty. I have dined
with her and Lord Charlemont in Grosvenor Street:
and have seen in their dining room the original
picture by Hogarth, "The Lady's Last Stake."

In the room in which the 1st Duke received his
guests at balls, there is a well known picture of Waterloo by Sir William Allan. I believe it was of this that
the Duke said "Very good! not too much smoke."
The painting is supposed to be taken from Napoleon's
position; and at the moment, when his last column
was advancing. Other incidents are represented, which
occurred during the day; but certainly not at the
same time. In this room is a poor portrait of Sir
Thomas Picton; and several more or less grotesque
representations of the Duke's friends; some of whose
names have disappeared from history. Colonel Gurwood, the Duke's Secretary, and Editor of his Dispatches, is there in a curious dress. It is that of
Squire to the Duke as a Knight of the Bath. In the
room used for the supper-room at the Duke's balls,

are several portraits of European Sovereigns, presented by them to him : none of the slightest merit.
The poor Emperor of Austria with his red pantaloons
appears to be in the last stage of decrepitude.

Over the chimney-piece in the supper-room is a
terrible portrait of George IV., almost so bad as that
of William IV., in another room, by Wilkie. I do not
know which is the most grotesque. King William is
strapped down ; with enormous spurs ; and looking as
miserable as a jovial sailor would do in a General's
uniform. George IV. is depicted in a dress, the most
picturesque in the world, if worn by a well-shaped
man, with a good leg and foot : these the King had ;
but Wilkie has contrived to make the portrait revolting.

George IV., as is well known, attended a ball at
Holyrood Palace dressed as a Highlander. His
Majesty had become corpulent at the time ; and could
hardly have "set off" the dress : but he made the
mistake of wearing a coat of the same tartan as the
kilt. This might have been done with good effect by
Prince Charles Edward, who was a handsome young
man ; but the simplicity of the tartan material is
quite unsuited to the velvet cuffs, embroidered with
gold, which George IV. added to it. The sporan is
too small and short, and should have been dark ;

not white. The hose, of the Royal colours, red and white, are unbecoming in themselves; but instead of reaching to three inches below the knee, as good sense and art would dictate, they are fastened round the centre of His Majesty's calves; and Wilkie has not even given him a good foot; which he certainly had to the last. The kilt is too short: indeed it would be difficult to find a much worse work of art in the history of Portraiture; and that is saying a good deal.

We have all read that at a subsequent ball, also in the Gallery of Kings at Holyrood, Sir William Curtis, a plethoric Alderman of London, appeared also in a kilt; to the boundless disgust of His Majesty; with whose person, of course, disagreeable comparisons were made.

The silver-gilt statue of the Duke by Alfred Count d'Orsay in this room is good. Criticism has been passed upon it that he has reduced the horse's flanks too much. In this statue the Duke wears the sword which I have described elsewhere as having been given him in India. The sword itself is contained in one of the horizontal cases of swords below. It is of distinctly Oriental character, and has a somewhat convex scabbard.

LIBRARY OF THE UNIVERSITY OF CALIFORNIA

Descending to the ground floor I asked if we could see the Duke's bedroom. The housekeeper replied that we could see it; but that it was no longer in the same condition in which it originally had been. When the 2nd Duke showed me over Apsley House, he pointed out his father's bedroom. It could hardly be dignified by the name of room; it was a closet. This closet is gone; but I found the precise spot where the bedstead stood. The bed was one that had belonged to Napoleon; and was in the style of the Empire. Anyone, in the least taller than the Duke, could not have laid at full length upon it; it looked very uncomfortable : the head of the bed was close to the half-door, which still exists, outside which is a small balcony directly leading to the garden. I hope that this spot may not be lost sight of; I am perfectly certain as to the locality. This room, in the north-west corner of which the closet existed, containing the bedstead, is now known as the "Garden Room." The rooms now built beyond it were, I believe, at the time of my earlier visit, occupied by the stables.

I was much struck with the excellence of the book-cases in the Library. They seemed to me not only in refined taste; but to be admirably suited for their purpose. I hope that the Duke of Wellington may be induced to place a small label upon every item of furniture in the house that belonged to his grandfather. It will make them priceless.

I induced my school-fellow, Mr. Webb of Newstead, to do this with the articles that had belonged to Lord Byron, and I am pleased to know that he did so.

I was invited to a party at Apsley House on what, in a small way, was an historical occasion. It was the first night on which Disraeli wore the Garter. He had, of course, as well the broad ribbon and the star; the latter made of magnificent diamonds presented to him by Sir Richard Wallace, who had inherited the star from Lord Hertford.

THE DUKE detested being helped; not from Ingratitude; but from two distinct feelings; one that he did not like to be thought, what he certainly was not, decrepit; the other that he knew very well that the majority of persons who helped him simply did so in order to be able to say that they had done so. This was to him revolting. Standing opposite to Apsley House in the evening in Piccadilly, when the street was even more crowded than it is now, the Duke was hesitating on the curbstone. A gentleman nearly so old as himself, made some demonstration of assisting him to cross the road; endeavouring to check the tide of cabs and other vehicles that was setting strongly. When the Duke reached the gate of Apsley House, he touched his hat; and said "I thank you, Sir." The elderly stranger immediately uncovered: holding his hat at his knee, he addressed the Duke as follows: "My Lord, I have passed a long, and not uneventful life; but never did I hope to reach the day when I might be of the slightest assistance to the greatest man that ever lived." The Duke looked at him calmly; and in a voice, not in the least choked by emotion, replied "Don't be a damned fool!" and walked into Apsley House.

I WAS ON DUTY with the Guard of Honour of the 1st Life-Guards at the lying-in-state of the Duke at Chelsea Hospital; on, what was called, "the select day." I believe that there were not more than thirteen thousand persons admitted. We marched from the Hyde Park Barracks in the early morning. It was blowing a gale, from the east; and the men were cloaked. We were ordered to wear our cuirasses, though dismounted; and I need hardly say that a Lifeguardsman, in full uniform, and wearing a heavy cloak, is an object upon which the wind may operate with telling effect : when we were crossing Sloane Square I thought my squadron would be blown out to sea. However we weathered the gale. The dress which the Officers wore, possibly from being unusual, I thought very picturesque. A broad black silk weeper covered the front of the helmet, and hung down the back. A black silk scarf crossed the cuirass from the shoulder to the hip ; and our gauntlets, instead of being white, were black. Our swords held all day with the point downwards. The room in which the Duke's coffin was placed was too small for so great an occasion. A sort of bedstead lighted up with numerous candles, sconces etc. was, I should say, copied from an old print of Marlborough's Lying-in-State. There seemed to me a want of Simplicity ; and in its place an amount of gewgaw which was not in character with either the circumstances, or the man. Being a Member of Parliament, I was not on duty with my Regiment at the Duke's funeral : so I had an opportunity of witnessing the Procession as well as the Ceremony in St Paul's. The Course of the Procession was along the Mall, Constitution Hill, Piccadilly, Pall Mall and thence westward. Contrary

to expectation the day was beautifully fine. I rode
from the Hyde Park Barracks, wearing the uniform
of the 1st Life Guards, when not on duty; and met
the procession near Buckingham Palace. I waited
near Stafford House to see them pass; rode on; and,
when I arrived at the foot of the Duke of York's
steps, found that what might have been a serious
difficulty had occurred. I had noticed, when going
off guard a few days before, that the little gutter
which runs to the west of the Duke of York's steps
in the Park, had been covered with new gravel. This
was soft: and the result, as might have been expected,
was that the enormously massive car, weighing many
tons, stood still. No amount of exertion could produce the slightest movement. One of the standard-
bearers, Lieutenant-Colonel Purvis, Equerry to the
Duchess of Cambridge, finding that the car was
immovable, asked me to ride back and tell the Officer
Commanding at the head of the column that the
procession must halt. I accordingly galloped off
along the Mall, through Stafford House Gate, up St
James's Street, and along Piccadilly, telling each of
the Officers Commanding Brigades what had happened. I then returned down Constitution Hill;
and was glad to find that the car had been moved;

and had already gone some way towards its destination.

Anything more impressive than the reception which the Duke's body received cannot be imagined. Few of the millions of London but contrived to see some part of it. Every atom of space, that could be utilized, was occupied. The bands at intervals played Handel's magnificent "Dead March"; as also Beethoven's, "On the Death of a Hero"; the former producing by far the finer effect. I rode through Whitehall to the river-steps near the House of Commons: sent back my horse: and by the steamboat, which was waiting there, reached St Paul's Chain. Thence I walked up to the Cathedral; finding my place among other Members of the House of Commons, some ' time before the procession arrived. The dome of the Cathedral was lighted with gas; and black curtains had been drawn over the windows, so that the light from above might be thrown on to the coffin; the remainder of the Cathedral being in gloom. Unfortunately for the effect the day turned out brilliant. I remember while we were waiting seeing Count Walewski, the French Ambassador, standing up conspicuously among the diplomatic corps; so that everyone might see him. This was no doubt done at the wise suggestion of the reigning Emperor of the French. The service, always beautiful, was well performed; and the fine chapter from the Epistle to the Corinthians being read by the Poet Dean Milman, the coffin was lowered; the effect of the " Dead March " in Saul, on the organ, was very poor. It could be scarcely heard; the organist, by way of being pathetic, playing it too piano. There should have been a large band in the Cathedral to play this glorious melody.

The following admirably written Article from the " Times " of November 18th, 1852, made a great impression on me at the time.

" Before the most honourable tomb this country can give closes over the remains of our great General and Statesman, our old and faithful servant and support, it is natural to pause, and cast yet another lingering retrospect on the career about to be so gloriously closed. Much has been written on this fruitful theme, but few can fail to observe that the sterling, and genuine character of the Duke of WELLINGTON gains more by careful, and critical analysis than by the most brilliant bursts of rhetoric, or best sustained flights of fancy. Let us, then, before we give to the Past one who was so lately a Mighty Presence among us, cast once more a glance over that wondrous life, and trace out the causes of his Greatness, and our Regret. Who can tell what would have been the state of Europe, or of England during the last half century, or at this moment, had ARTHUR WELLESLEY never lived; or had his fate been cut short by the bullet, or the sabre under the walls of Seringapatam?

"Without the slightest personal ostentation, with a simplicity of character utterly alien from display, or egotism, such was the force of his talents, and the vigour of his energies, that he became the life, and soul of every transaction in which he took part; and the prominent figure in almost every one of the long series of historical pictures in which he must always be included. It is ever difficult to separate the history of the Campaign from the biography of the General, but in the campaigns of the Duke of WELLINGTON they become absolutely identical. Cool; cautious; daring; and indefatigable; now FABIUS and now MARCELLUS, he preserved in either capacity the same mind; which Adversity could not depress nor Prosperity elate; the same self-sacrificing caution, which checked the ardour of an

I

advance; and the same firm, and unbounded re-
liance in his own Genius, and in the valour of his
troops, which often wrung Victory out of retreat; and
converted a momentary disaster into a permanent
triumph. Without him there would probably have
been no Assaye: without him there would certainly
have been no Waterloo. The same quick glance,
and unfaltering hardihood detected in both the possibility of Victory amid the elements of danger. Yet
this daring man was not more daring than cautious.
The masterly retreat into Portugal; the lines of
Torres Vedras; and the advance into the South of
France, all testify that the one quality was as natural
to him as the other. Unlike ordinary campaigners,
the whole events of the War he conducted bear the
impress of his single mind: and our interest is, in
spite of ourselves, concentrated on the General.

"Nor should it be forgotten, in estimating the
claims of this greatest of our warriors to our Gratitude and Respect, that the Duke of WELLINGTON
had to create the Military System under which he
conquered; and which he has bequeathed to us.
The complete system of the Commissariat which
facilitated so much the operations of his later Campaigns, was the creation of his untiring diligence:

the painful result of his unremitting labour. He found our army a disorganized mass : he left it, at the end of the Peninsular War, an instrument of destruction as complete and efficient as Genius ever framed, or skill ever wielded.

"Nothing that related to the comfort of the soldier was to him a matter of indifference. His method of cooking ; the time, and manner of receiving his pay, and many other things, which to ordinary minds would appear below the dignity of the heroic stature, were objects of constant attention to him, while he was manœuvring in the face of a powerful and skilful enemy ; was striving to animate his allies with his own spirit; cajoling half a dozen obstinate, and intriguing Juntas; checking the anxiety of the English Ministry for a little bloodshed, to help them through the Parliamentary Campaign ; advising Spain on the treatment of her revolted colonies ; and entering into financial speculations to obtain funds for the payment of his Army.

"Without this spirit, which could dare everything and endure everything; which could grasp the mightiest events ; yet not neglect the smallest details, it is indeed difficult to conceive how the Peninsular War could have been carried on to a successful termination. The Duke of WELLINGTON alone of all whom history mentions soared superior to mere good fortune; and impressed upon the proceedings of the day the unvarying stamp of his own Vigilance, and Genius. We are, therefore, justified in concluding that we we were successful because we had him for our Commander: that he was not carried on by an irresistible tide of events; but made for himself those opportunities which he knew so well how to improve.

" If this was not also the case in his Political Career, it was probably because he had to deal with events over which no individual mind can exercise a commanding influence; but even here, dangers, which he could not avert were clearly foreseen; justly appreciated; and prudently met. The Simplicity, Uprightness, and Massiveness of his character, free from all those perplexing influences of Vanity, Passion, Irresolution, or Selfishness which blind the vision of ordinary mortals, gave his firm, and impassible glance a peculiar and inexplicable intuition into the immediate results of every conjuncture of affairs, civil or military. The medium was clear, solid, and without a flaw; and the refraction was free from distortion, or the delusive brilliancy of prismatic colouring.

"A want of the imaginative faculty rendered him it is true, a just, rather than a farsighted, observer, but if the range of mental vision was limited, the vision within those limits was exquisitely, and unerringly correct. Like THEMISTOCLES, he could foresee the better, and the worse: and, like him, by the mere effort of natural Genius he could always strike out the course that ought to be adopted. Such a power, limited as it was to the more immediate results of existing conjunctures, was the highest perfection of the Practical Intellect; had it extended to more remote contingencies, it would have been, not Intuition, but Inspiration.

"Almost the only good fortune we can ascribe to this extraordinary man was, that his position in life gave him, in common with thousands of others, who are gone down to the grave unremembered, an easy access to the sphere of Command, and Activity; and that his mental qualities were such as eminently qualified him to be of the utmost service to his country, in an age of War from without, and of Faction and Tumult from within. If his Caution, and Valour repeatedly saved us from the most imminent danger, his Wisdom, Patriotism, and Moderation preserved us at least as frequently from internal

discord : perhaps from Revolution. The very nar-
rowness of the political school in which he was
educated probably served his Country just as effectually as his more brilliant qualifications. A man
more desirous of Popularity, more open to Impulse,
more carried away by Imagination, and Feeling,
would never have obtained that hold over the minds
of the Aristocracy which the Duke of WELLING-
TON so frequently exerted at critical and dangerous
moments.

"A weak man advising concession; a timid man
advocating conciliation; or a vain man speaking on
the popular side, would have carried but little weight:
but when the strong, the bold, and single-minded
soldier counselled peace, and compromise, it would
have argued desperate rashness in the House of Peers
to have resisted the opinion of one whose Judgment
was never swayed by fear; and whose Wisdom never
courted, nor shunned the applause of the multitude.
How often has the Duke of WELLINGTON inter-
posed between his own Order and its Passions and
Prejudices! How often has the dauntless soldier
been the advocate and counsellor of Peace!

"Nothing shows more clearly the intellectual
stature of the man than the undoubted fact that,

bowed down as he was by the unceasing toils of more than eighty years, he was, up to the last moment of his life, not only a mighty Memory and Glorious Record of the heroic past, but an actual Power whose existence every one knew; and whose intervention the Country was ready at any moment to invoke. Having survived the Generals, the Subalterns, and the Armies he commanded, his friends, his colleagues, and his subordinates in office, he still remained the Great Mediator between the conflicting powers of the State; the adviser of the Crown; and the moderator of the Peers.

"But he is gone; suddenly, though not prematurely, with his years and his honours: and where shall we find the man who can in the slightest degree fill the void which a Personage so august has left behind him?

"There has been but one such subject since England was a Monarchy; and a wonderful combination of circumstances must occur before there can be such another. We are not of those who underrate the existing generation of men, in order to render exaggerated, and often undeserved, honour to their predecessors. There is not another actor on the political scene whose place cannot be supplied:

but never the place once filled by ARTHUR WEL-
LESLEY. Truly we may say to those who would
treat the death of THE DUKE as a theme for
reviving old party dissensions; who contrast his
political with his military career; and introduce the
paltry criticism of partisanship into their estimate of
a character too vast to be held in the bonds of
faction, even as DAVID said when they told him of
the death of ABNER—' Know ye not that a Prince,
and a Great Man has fallen this day in Israel?'"

AS JOHNSON has wisely said, " Patriotism," (sham
Patriotism, "the good of his country") "is the last
refuge of the scoundrel." The Duke's patriotism was
pure. So consummate was his Honesty that the somewhat feeble question put by him "How is the King's
Government to be carried on?" did not bring any
imputation upon his good faith.

Of course to a Statesman this question is hardly an
argument. The duty of a Statesman is to do his best
to carry on the King's Government; and at the same
time to withstand noxious measures. The Duke ultimately surrendered his position in relation to any
measure; however much he disapproved : and, wonderful to relate, he openly declared to his enemies

that he expected that they would beat him. His well known statement in the House of Lords in relation to Civil War was founded upon Knowledge, and Generosity; but his declaration that he would sacrifice his life sooner than see his beloved country plunged into Civil War for one month, however admirable in sentiment, was surely Imprudence itself; at any rate it certainly led to his defeat.

ON ONE OCCASION a member of the King's Cabinet apologizing to the rest for not knowing so much as many of them, the Duke turned to him; and said "Don't apologize: you know quite as much as you can digest."

I HAVE ALLUDED to the saying "What a shocking bad hat." There was another phrase known in my childhood; "No mistake."

Everyone added to what they had said "and no mistake." "There is a fine horse, 'and no mistake;'" "There is a fine woman 'and no mistake;'" "That was a fine speech 'and no mistake;'" "I am quite ready 'and no mistake;'" "He has got it now 'and no mistake;'" etc. etc. ad infinitum.

This saying, apparently unmeaning, originated in the following circumstance. Mr. Huskisson, the eminent statesman, being a member of the Government of which the Duke was the head, voted in the Opposition lobby, on a Division in the House of Commons. The Duke who had no idea of Insubordination, wrote to the wanderer at once to say that the Sovereign would accept Mr. Huskisson's resignation. Mr. Huskisson wrote back to say that he had received the Duke's letter; and that " there must be some mistake." The Duke answered in his usual terse style "There is no mistake : there has been no mistake : and there shall be no mistake ; " and out went Mr. Huskisson. This became known, and gave rise to the slang saying.

I WAS INTRODUCED to the Duke by my mother at an evening party at Lady Laura Meyrick's, 30 Curzon Street, May Fair. The Duke shook hands with me very kindly. I leant forward and said distinctly " Your Grace may possibly remember my father, Sir James Fraser?" He answered "I remember him perfectly : in the 7th Hussars." His manner, particularly to young people, was always most gratifying. He always seemed pleased : and though frequent presentations must have bored him, he never showed this in his manner.

THE 1ST AND 2ND Duke both had the same defect, a most uncomfortable one; their tongues being too large for their mouths; this made them both occasionally inarticulate. The 1st Duke overcame this defect by placing the point of the tongue so low down as possible in the mouth. This gave a cavernous, and peculiar sound. The Duke's voice when addressing the House of Lords was most sonorous; and never to be forgotten.

THERE IS NO SUBJECT relating to the termination of the Great War, upon which more bitter things have been said than the execution of the Prince of the Moscowa. I have no wish here to go into the circumstances which lead to his death; but there was one person who unquestionably was grossly wronged in the affair, and that was the Duke of Wellington. All the Envy and Malice which had accumulated during his brilliant, and honest career was poured upon him at this juncture. It has been said a hundred times that he could have saved Ney's life had he chosen to do so. He went every possible

length with the King's Ministers to induce them to
spare the life of one of the bravest soldiers that ever
lived. He found his remonstrances were vain : he
then endeavoured to approach the King personally
on the subject. Louis XVIII., who knew perfectly
well what the Duke wished, showed him gross rude-
ness on the occasion when he attempted to ask
him to spare Ney's life ; and the Duke felt that it
was impossible to do more. Foolish, shallow, and
malignant people have declared that such were the
obligations of Louis XVIII. to the Duke that he
must have obeyed his slightest hint. Nothing more
absurd can be conceived. The very fact of the
boundless obligations which the King of France was
under to his restorer put them upon more or less
distant terms. The 2nd Duke told me more than
once that his father said to him often that whatever
Ney deserved, he had done his utmost to prevent
his execution.

Ney's infatuation in refusing the tribunal of Marshals,
four of whom were his own comrades, and insisting
upon being tried by the House of Peers, teeming at
that time with political excitement, and rancour,
brought about his fate. In appointing the Marshals
to try him, I shall always believe that the French

Government wished to get out of a difficult situation ;
but in spite of the advice of his excellent, and
chivalrous friend, and advocate, Berryer, the Prince
of the Moscowa absolutely refused any tribunal but
that of the Peers. The first words that Berryer
addressed to him after the sentence were, "My poor
friend, you would have it so." The Duke never
in his life showed anything but a feeling of great
Humanity, great Forbearance ; and whatever he may
have thought of Ney's conduct, and let us remember
that Waterloo and its slaughter would not have taken
place had it not been for Ney's joining Napoleon,
he decidedly left no stone unturned to prevent his
death. Mr. Quentin Dick, who sat in the Irish Parliament, and after the Union, in the English Parliament for many years, whom I knew well, saw Marshal
Ney shot ; and described the execution to me.

His laquais de place told him, on the morning of
the fatal day, that Marshal Ney was to be shot in the
Gardens of the Luxembourg ; he immediately went
there. The weather was perfect ; and the gardens
were filled, as usual, with children, and nursery-maids.
He waited at the gate, where Ney's statue now is ;
and where a wall then stood. A fiacre drove up,
containing the Marshal, an officer of Gendarmerie,

and two sergeants. The four stepped out of the
carriage. The officer beckoned to the picket of
soldiers stationed on duty at the gate. Marshal Ney
was dressed in a black surtout, white neck-cloth, with
crape round his hat; he was in mourning at the time
for (I think) his father-in-law; dark pantaloons, and
Hessian boots. He wore no decoration. He was
placed against the wall, uttered a few words which
Mr. Quentin Dick could not hear; the picket fired;
and the Marshal fell on his face. The body was at
once placed in the fiacre; which drove off; the
whole transaction not occupying three minutes. It
was all over before the nurses, and the children
could realize what had happened.

The official account is evidently a fabrication; for it
says that the body of the late Prince of the Moscowa
was allowed, according to law, to remain a quarter of
an hour in a public thoroughfare. This, in itself, is
of course absurd. Half Paris would have been there.
I confess to have yet a lingering doubt whether Ney
was shot to death. Some years afterwards, on the
death of the Duke de Reichstadt, a gentleman residing
in North America, bearing a name which I at this
moment forget, connected with that of Michael Ney,
(I rather think it was his mother's name), hearing of

the death of Napoleon's son, exclaimed "Then my last hope is gone." He never alluded to the subject of his birth, nor history, either before or after that moment: but there were people at the time of his death who insisted that he might have been the great soldier, the Prince of the Moscowa, and Duke of Elchingen; and, as he himself said while the fatal sentence was being read to him, "Michel Ney: very soon a few handfuls of dust." Nothing would be more consistent with the Duke's truly great character than this willingness to bear all the abuse, the slander, the venom, of the commonplace wretches who yelled at him; and to know the whole time that the man was not dead; and, as a matter of Honour, to carry the secret with him to his grave.

The 2nd Duke told me, in the same conversation, of a scene that occurred at Windsor Castle; a scene very much to be regretted. Having been invited by the Queen to dine there to meet the Emperor and Empress of the French, who were on a visit, while coffee was being handed round after dinner, the Emperor led up to the Duke Marshal Ney's son, who was of his suite. The latter did not know him, which seems surprizing from the Duke's striking resemblance to his father; and wearing his star, garter etc.

The Emperor said "I must introduce two great
names." **The Duke** made a low bow. The Emperor
observing that General Ney did not know the Duke,
whispered to him; whereupon Marshal Ney's son
clearly indicated that he did not wish to make the
Duke's acquaintance. It seems a pity that this feeling
should continue so long; particularly under the circumstances which I have mentioned : that the Duke
not only had nothing to do with the condemnation of
the unfortunate Marshal ; but did everything to save
his life.

So determined was the King, and those about him,
to prevent the Duke having any opportunity of personally asking that Ney's life should be spared, that
not only did Louis XVIII. turn his back upon the
Duke, when he approached him ; but the Comte
d'Artois placed himself between the Duke and the
King. The Duke felt this insult very much : and,
openly, and very properly, showed his resentment.
After Marshal Ney was shot, and their object was
attained, **every effort** was made on the part of the
French Royal Family to reconcile the Duke to the
King. The **Comte d'Artois**, afterwards Charles X.,
called upon the Duke; and begged him, almost on
his knees, to visit the King. The Duke sternly

refused : pointing out that he knew perfectly well the motives that had influenced the Comte d'Artois, and others. For some time he abstained from all approach to the Sovereign.

.At length, possibly from political necessities, he consented to an interview with the King on business ; but I believe that he showed to the last how deeply he felt the indignity to which he had been exposed.

For the abuse lavished upon him by envious minds he cared nothing; but I know that, to the last, he felt deeply the base requital which he had.received at the hands of those to whom he had given a kingdom.

The 2nd Duke of Wellington told me these facts more than once.

AMONG THOSE who joined in the cry against the Duke was one who, for many reasons, ought to have known better; one who had himself met with Calumny ; and who had been socially proscribed; not because he was wickeder than many of his accusers ; but because he was infinitely cleverer. When Lord Byron wrote his abusive lines on the Duke of Wellington, he disgraced himself. They degraded him: and belied his Genius. Lord Byron in another place had written lines that will never perish. The beautiful lines

K

"He who surpasses or subdues Mankind
Must look down on the Hate of those below,"

are true.

Well might he have taken example from the Duke as to what a man's conduct should be under such circumstances.

On this, as on every other occasion of his life, the unbending dignity of the Duke was conspicuous: and one regrets not to have seen more of this real superiority in the mental characteristics of Lord Byron.

A CURIOUS INCIDENT occurred at the time when Mr. Tylney Wellesley, afterwards 4th Earl of Mornington, who by marrying an heiress, acquired a number of other names, was Master of the Mint. He caused a certain number of shillings to be struck, on which the letters "T. W." were placed on the lower edge of the Sovereign's neck. George IV. found this out: and was extremely angry. I believe those shillings are at a considerable premium at this time. I have seen one.

THE 2nd DUKE told me that in examining his

father's papers, of which there was an enormous accumulation, he observed that, except in the earlier ones, the first paragraph was not headed with the figure 1. He conceived that this might have been from carelessness : but he ascertained from some memorandum that the Duke had done it intentionally. Indeed, as a matter of good sense, any number would be superfluous at the beginning of a document; the other numbers 2. 3. 4. etc., being carefully placed to mark the separation.

I HAVE ALWAYS THOUGHT that the Duke, at the time of the difficulty with Queen Caroline, formed a very sound, and, I am sure, a not ill-natured opinion relating to her. It appears from a book lately published that so far from the Queen having been excluded from Westminster Abbey, arrangements were made at each door for her admission : and a pew, or reserved seat, was kept for her. The R⁺ Hon. George Bankes, of Kingston Lacy, who held office in Lord Derby's Government in 1852, told me that, as a Page, he witnessed what took place on the Queen's arrival at the Abbey. Her carriage stopped at the small gate leading to Poet's Corner, immediately opposite to the House of Lords. The Queen, with her Lady-in-

Waiting, and Lord Hood, walked up the narrow passage between the railings; and at the actual door of the Abbey was received by some official, whose duty it was to inspect the tickets of persons admitted. He said that this person may or may not have known the Queen by sight: few people did. The official gentleman said to the Queen "Madam, I must ask you for your ticket." The reply was "I don't require a ticket: I am the Queen." The official made a very low bow; and looking at the Lady-in-Waiting said "I must ask this lady for her ticket." None was produced. The Queen turned to Lord Hood; and said "My Lord, what do you advise?" After a short pause, Lord Hood said "I really cannot advise your Majesty." Queen Caroline hesitated: looked distressed: then walked slowly back to her carriage. The Guard of Honour, which had received her with Royal honours, again presented arms; and she drove off. Not much excitement was caused in the crowd. These statements are not altogether inconsistent. Had she persevered in going into the Abbey, a place no doubt would have been kept for her: and I should think that the Duke's generalship would have enabled him to take care that no unseemly interruption of the august ceremony took place.

AT THE TIME when every effort was being made
to enlist public sympathy with Queen Caroline, various
devices were resorted to : among others, sending
deputations to Brandenburg House, Hammersmith;
where the Queen was residing. It was anxiously
wished to enlist the sympathies of the Scottish nation
on her side : and as a means of doing this

> " Five hundred Mile Enders
> Dressed up as Highlanders "

were marched to her house: and courteously received.

LORD REDESDALE told me the following story
shortly before his death. It was felt by the deep and
earnest portion of the population that a great effect
would be produced if the Charity Children of London
attended the Queen; and expressed to her Majesty
their conviction that she was perfectly innocent. It
will be remembered that Lord Denman, after an elo-
quent, and final harangue in defence of the Queen,
after protesting for a day that her Majesty's character
was spotless, terminated his speech in this remarkable
manner : he entreated the House of Lords to follow
the example of One, whose name is too sacred to be
here inserted ; and implored the Peers to say to her

Majesty " Go, and sin no more." This excited some derision among his professional brothers; however, the passage was thought not unworthy of being turned into a Hymn. Accordingly the innocent children, who were assembled in front of Brandenburg House, the Queen being on the balcony, addressed her in the following verse, set to a well-known psalm tune:

"Gracious Lady! we implore
You will go, and sin no more:
Or, if the effort be too great,
Go away at any rate !"

LORD M., who is now living, has told me that he remembers the Queen's entrance into London.

The mob surrounded her carriage; exclaiming vociferously "God bless your Majesty; we know you are innocent; God bless your innocent son." This allusion being to William Austin, who was in the carriage. George IV. seems to have been most annoyed by Alderman Wood sitting next to the Queen.

In her delirium before death, Queen Caroline never alluded to her alleged accomplice.

IT HAS BEEN said of the Duke that he was asked

what were the rules for a good speaker in public : this is a mistake. The Duke was asked whether he had rules for his own speaking : he said "Only two : one is I never speak about what I know nothing ; and the other I never quote Latin." With his imperfect recollection of Latin quantities, the latter rule, as well as the former, showed his good sense.

THE DUKE had a high opinion of Marlborough, which he generously expressed. When asked who was the greatest General in history, nothing would have been easier than to say Napoleon ; the sequitur being, of course, that he had beaten him ; and therefore that he was greater. He took care to point out how the Duke of Marlborough had been thwarted by the States-General ; and by his other Allies. When reminded that the English Government had refused him what he wanted, at least according to the popular impression, he generously replied "No ; they always yielded when I pressed them."

THE DUKE escaped one great source of Envy, which accounted for some of the venom with which Marlborough was attacked. The Duke was not a

beauty. Marlborough was the handsomest man of
his day. No one could possibly say of the Duke
that his was an ugly face; teeming with character,
and with good features, one would certainly put him
on the beauty side of the line.

THE DUKE had always the greatest contempt for
the worthlessness of the public opinion of the moment.
The "ignorant present" he considered beneath
notice. He felt that he was doing, and had done, his
duty. He trusted that ultimately Justice would be
done him: and, if it were not, he could bear the
wrong philosophically.

IN THESE DAYS every thing is done by exami-
ations. Whether the examinations prove much is a
doubtful question. They are the means of getting rid
of many candidates for the Army. I have heard it
said that a vivâ voce examination is not fair upon
a young man; and that, what at Oxford we call "paper
work" should be used for military examinations. I
hold exactly a contrary opinion. They say that a
young man may be unnerved by being asked questions
vivâ voce. That is exactly one of the things that you
wish to test. If a man has half an hour to think

how to answer a question, that is one thing. If he is obliged to answer it instantly, it is another: no better test could be applied as regards intellectual nerve, which a soldier requires, than a vivâ voce examination; particularly at Oxford, where, in former days, three mistakes were sufficient to turn you out of the Schools. I sincerely hope that vivâ voce examinations will never be done away with. What is wanted in an Officer is to have ready, and instantaneous Resource.

The Duke preferred an University graduate to all other officers : there are several monuments in Christ Church Cathedral to graduates killed in action.

IT IS SAID that the Duke avoided reading histories of himself; lest he should have to contradict them; very possibly, this was the case; except in instances where facts were brought officially before him.

HIS LONG RELUCTANCE to grant a Medal to the veterans of the Peninsular War at first seems harsh. One must suppose that he felt that the intricate questions of individuality involved would be insuper- able. The identity of the soldiers' names, and the various, and complicated circumstances under which different Regiments were engaged, would no doubt have led to very great difficulties. I believe that he gave this as a reason for his objection. Still, it seems a pity that when the heart of the nation was honourably, and justly set upon this, he did not show a greater willingness to accede to the request. The concession was ultimately brought about entirely by the personal exertions of the late Duke of Richmond, who deserves every credit for fighting the battle of the Old Soldiers.

Knowing, as one does, the great value that soldiers attach to these things, it must have been very hard for a man, who had been through a dozen severely fought battles in the Peninsula, to see a youth half his age, who had smelt powder for the first time at Waterloo, wearing a decoration; while he, having lost possibly a limb or an eye, should have nothing to show for his long services.

THE DUKE no doubt was occasionally angry, and probably with just cause, at the careless conduct of his Regimental Officers; but their behaviour at Waterloo, many of them never having been in action before, roused the enthusiasm even of his philosophical nature. He describes them behaving as if they were playing at cricket. Most of us have read the well

known passage in Montalembert, where he describes
the Duke as saying "The battle of Waterloo was won
in the playing fields of Eton." The manliness of
that great school told upon his Officers.

THE DUKE said that Strathfieldsaye, which seems
to have been bought in a hurry, in order to be presented to him, would have ruined any other man.

APSLEY HOUSE, which has been called "No. 1.
London," was, when purchased for the Duke, of red
brick; and belonged, I believe, to Lord Bathurst.
Like most corner houses, it is, I should say, a
cold house in the winter; three sides being exposed:
but it is bright and cheerful; the situation very
healthy; and easy of access to the Parks and the
west end of London generally.

NO MAN EVER EXTORTED Admiration, without much valuing it, more than the Duke of Wellington. Johnson wisely says in his preface to
Shakespeare "How easy is it to obtain Praise for
him whom no man may envy!" The Duke's
character triumphed over this. He forced Mankind, as it were, to their knees: and, in the end,

they could no more shut their eyes to his greatness than obscure the light of the sun at noon.

I HAVE SAID that Sarah Lady Jersey was an intimate friend of the Duke. Becoming Lady Grandison in 1804, her husband succeeded to his higher title in 1805 : from that time to the day of her death in 1867 she was absolute Queen of London Society. She never had a real rival. Frances Anne, Lady Londonderry, sister-in-law of the great Castlereagh ; and wife of a distinguished soldier, was richer ; had higher rank ; a much larger house ; and was, in her own person, the representative of an ancient, and wealthy family ; and devoted herself, to a great extent, to Society. She never had such Sovereignty.

Lady Palmerston, the wife of one Prime Minister, the sister of another ; most beautiful in her youth, and handsome to the last, held a high position in London Society : but from circumstances, principally political, she never showed the same exclusiveness as Lady Jersey. Lord Palmerston being more closely connected with our political system, she was, of course, not so absolutely a free agent ; and, though fastidious in her choice, she was more or less compelled to bend to necessity.

Lady Jersey never was a beauty. She had a grand figure to the last ; never became the least corpulent ; and, to use a common term, there was obviously no " make up " about her. A considerable mass of grey hair: dressed not as a young woman, but as a middle-aged one : entirely in this, as in other things, without Affectation, her appearance was always pleasant. No trace of rouge, nor dye could ever be seen about her. She had natural, simple manners, as a Grande Dame ought to have. She seemed to take her Sovereignty as a matter of course : to be neither vain of it; nor, indeed, to think much about it. Very quick, and intelligent; with the strongest sense of humour that I have ever seen in woman ; taking the keenest delight in a good joke ; and having, I should say, great physical enjoyment of life ; yet, withal, few went through greater family misfortunes than she did ; surviving all her children. It would be a great mistake to suppose that she was a person of hard, or unfeeling disposition. I have seen her more than once under circumstances that disproved this. I remember a day's journey round Beauly Firth which I took with Evan Baillie of Dochfour, Lady Jersey, and her daughter. We kept up cheery conversation all day long ; and a very amusing day it was. Towards evening, by some chance, an allusion was made to her son, Augustus Villiers, usually known, why I know not, as " Jack Villiers"; who died at Rome.   From that moment I observed Lady Jersey's manner change. She hardly said anything : and, leaning back in the carriage, I saw the tears, under her veil, rolling down her cheeks.   I believe that hers was one of those healthy, and elastic natures upon which Grief, al-though weighing heavily at the time, as with children, does not produce a lasting impression.

Lady Jersey was very intimate with Disraeli, who admired her intellectually, and philosophically ; and paints her in at least one of his novels.   It was to her that the Duke gave his opinion the day before he left the Premiership, not to return, " Oh, we're all right : we're not going out."   Lady Jersey in-herited a considerable fortune and a share in Child's bank under peculiar circumstances ; well known at the time, now almost forgotten.   Mr Child, the Banker, who purchased, and furnished in the most perfect taste, the house at Osterley Park, near Brent-ford, had an only daughter ; heiress presumptive to his wealth.   Almost immediately after he had com-pleted his house, filling it with every beautiful object that he could collect of the Taste, and Style of the last century, his daughter, a most beautiful girl, eloped with Lord Burghersh, the eldest son of the Lord Westmorland of that day.

I can remember this smart young officer, when very old, and totally blind, riding at a smart trot along the crowded cliff at Brighton: he is depicted by H.B. in his Equestrian Sketches, as "Old Rapid."

This young nobleman, an Officer in the Guards, eloped with Miss Child for Gretna Green. The indignant father pursued them: so near was he to their capture ·that, but for the presence of mind of Lord Burghersh, he would have been able to prevent the marriage. When beyond Carlisle Mr Child was within a few yards of their post-chaise; Lord Burghersh leaning out of the window, fired his pistol, and struck one of the leaders of Mr Child's carriage between the fore legs. The horse staggered; and fell: and the couple were enabled to carry out their intention at Gretna Green, on crossing the border.

Mr Child however, was determined that although he could not deprive Lord Burghersh of his wife; he would effectually deprive him, and his family, of her fortune. He accordingly settled it upon any daughter that might be born of the marriage. The daughter that was born was Sarah Lady Jersey; who always remained a partner in Child's bank.

Osterley is a beautiful house. I have visited it during its occupation by Duchess William of Cleveland; who was an excellent tenant of Lord Jersey's for many years.

I discovered in the Library which was purchased by Mr Child about 1770, and no book of which had apparently been touched from that time, a perfect 'Faust's Bible'; and a parchment copy in manuscript with beautiful illuminations of Gower's "Confessio Amantis." These most valuable books, with many others, were lying absolutely unprotected; and at the mercy of any ignorant, and still more of any knowing, and crafty, individual. I begged that my hostess would point out the fact to the owner of the house : and they were afterwards protected by wire net.

The Collection was sold a few years ago; and fetched a very large sum; the two books I have mentioned fetching many hundreds. The furniture in every room in the house, of which, I believe, but very little has been removed, was the most perfect that could be bought at the time, 1770-1780. Every carpet, curtain, lamp, bedstead etc. were in the ideal perfection of that period; and many very valuable old pictures hang still in the bright sunny south gallery. The walls of one large square room are covered with beautiful French tapestry. This bears the date. The house, as is well known, was built by Sir Thomas Gresham : and on Queen Elizabeth visiting it, having at her entry remarked that it was a pity to divide the court-yard by a wall, her Majesty, on rising the next morning, found that her loyal subject had removed the impediment.

I have spoken of Lady Jersey's appearance. I remember Madame Collorédo, for many years Austrian Ambassadress in London, speaking to me of her at Nice soon after Lady Jersey's death. Some French ladies were in the room ; and the conversation was carried on in that language. She turned to them and said " I will tell you what Lady Jersey was. A quatre-vingt ans elle portait une robe décolletée ; et elle n'était pas choquante."

More remarkable than all ; during a long life, passed in a most scandalous age, no word was ever uttered against her character : this I know from those who saw her in Youth, and Prime.

LORD WELLLESLEY and the Duke of Wellington were at the same house at Eton. The rooms were in

my day in the same state as when occupied by the
Duke. The windows looked into the garden, through
which is the path to the front door. The house stands
across the road to the right, when you enter Eton
from the Slough road.

I received the following letter from one who could
not be mistaken in the matter :

"5th April, 1889.

"My dear Fraser.

"I can give you information about the Duke's
and Lord Wellesley's rooms at first hand : you are
quite right about their being the two rooms just inside
the door, and passage, between the boys' part and my
own part, on the first floor.

"When I was building the rooms at right angles to
the old house, I got Lord Hardinge to bring the
great Duke down to my house from the Castle ; and
to point out his room.

"The Duke made at once for the recess or lobby,
on the right hand of the passage. The Duke said
' That we called " Maidens' Bower," because the
"boys' maids " sat there at work every afternoon.'
His, and Lord Wellesley's rooms were opposite that.

"Accordingly, when I was pulling down a good

deal of the old house, I religiously preserved those two rooms.

"Further; I was told at the time by an old Etonian that the Duke's name had been seen in one of the rooms cut out on some of the panelling: I searched in vain for it.

"Thirty-five years after that, when I was staying with Provost Goodford at the Lodge, what should I see in his Drawing-room but a picture of the Duke, with a piece of a skirting board or panelling, with the name cut on it 'Wellesley min., 1784.'

"I said to the Provost 'What does this mean?' 'Oh,' he said, 'that board was found in the Duke's room in your old house.' I was obliged to say, 'Provost, you have been hoaxed: that was never cut out in 1784.' 'Why not?' said the Provost. 'Because in 1784 the Duke's name was "Wesley minimus," not Wellesley.'

"The old Dean of Windsor, Wellesley, was dining there: and I appealed to him. He gave it against me; and said he had never heard of it.

"A week later he wrote to say that he had been talking to the 2nd Duke of Wellington, who knew nothing of the Duke's being Wesley min. at that time. However, when he went to Strathfieldsaye he hunted up the papers; and found I was right. It was Lord Wellesley; who had changed his name five or six years before the Duke did."

In a subsequent letter, dated 7th of April, 1889, the same excellent authority says:

"I am grieved to say that when I last went to the old quarters to look about, I found that the Wellesley (or Wesley) rooms were demolished. I heard that it was not done by the present occupant."

Unless I am very much mistaken, I saw the cutting "Wellesley min." when I went to Eton.

THE ORIGIN of the well-deserved promotion of Chaplain-General Gleig is interesting. The Duke staying in a country house was, like other great men, reluctant to go to bed early. However, he retired with the rest of the company. Returning to the drawing room for a book, he saw lying on the table "The Subaltern." The Duke was pleased with the technical accuracy, and honesty, with which this book was written. He wrote to the publisher; and said that as it was obvious that the author of "The Subaltern" was an Officer, he would be very glad to assist him. The publisher replied that the author was a Clergyman, who had formerly served in a

Regiment of the Line; and that he held a curacy in
Kent. On the Duke becoming acquainted with M^r
Gleig, the latter said that he had always wished to be
made Chaplain to Chelsea Hospital. Later on this
was done : and he ultimately developed into Chaplain-General of the Forces. I have heard him preach
occasionally at Chelsea; and thought his style good;
simple; terse : with not unfrequent apostrophic appeals
to "Soldiers !" I cannot, however, quite forgive him
for his dullness about the Duke's bedstead, at Apsley
House.

Some one remarking to the Duke that no one could
turn in such a bed, he replied "When a man begins to
turn in his bed, it is time he should turn out." Gleig
mangles this: making the Duke say "When a man
begins to turn in his bed, it is time he should get up." !

I HAVE SAID that no portrait of the Duke was like
him. I had a very interesting conversation with the
2nd Duke on this subject. He said "I agree with you
that none of the portraits of my father are like him."
I said "I cannot account for the fact of every one
representing him with hollow, 'lantern,' cheeks; whereas his head was formed on the most beautiful lines ;
particularly the straight line from the temple to the

corner of the jaw : his was a fine, massive, symmetrical head ; only fit to be sculptured in granite ;
faultless in its proportions ; a head such as you don't
see twice in your life ; such he was, when I recollect
him." The Duke replied : " Yes, you are quite right!
I will tell you all about it. You may have observed that my father, when not speaking, had a
movement of his lips, as if he were chewing. That
arose from his artificial teeth not fitting him properly.
He lost all his back teeth early in life ; this was
the reason of the sunken condition of his cheeks.
It was only when he was compelled to wear a set of
artificial teeth that the natural configuration of his
head returned." It is impossible to get any idea of
his appearance from any of the portraits of him that
have been done. I have examined almost every
portrait of him, whether painted or engraved ; and not
one of them represent him in the least degree such as
I can perfectly recall him.

I have an original portrait in watercolours of him.

I HAD THE FOLLOWING from the widow of
the excellent churchman, whose name appears in the
story. When Dr Monk was Dean of Peterborough,
the Verger of the Cathedral said to him one day, after

Evening Week-day Service was over, "A Gentleman has been here this morning, Sir, who asked a great many questions." "Who was he?" "I don't know, Sir." "Where did he come from?" "I don't know, Sir: he was on horseback; and said to his groom: 'Take the horses outside the town; and don't chatter.' He went all over the Cathedral, and asked me a great deal about all sorts of things. When he went away, he said 'I wish your master had charge of all the Cathedrals in England; he'd save me a lot of trouble, I can tell you.'" A few months afterwards the Dean of Peterborough received a letter to the following effect:

"Mr Dean: Should it suit you, I shall be glad to recommend you to the King for the Bishopric of Gloucester, which has recently become vacant. Please to let me have your answer so soon as you can. Yours faithfully

"WELLINGTON."

AN AUTHENTIC STORY is told of a certain noble lord, whose name I will suppress; but who held at one time a very important political position. Being on duty at the Horse Guards with the Guard of the Household Cavalry, he had occasion to write

a note to the Duke of Wellington, who was in the
Commander in Chief's office closely adjacent. The
Duke looked at the address; and finding himself
designated on it as " Field Martial," asked with surprize where the note came from; without opening
it. He was told from the Officer commanding the
Guard of the Blues. The Duke sent the note back
with the intimation that Captain —— had made a
mistake in the address. Another note was promptly
brought to the Duke, in which the word " Martial "
had been changed into a word, representing the senior
member of a well known firm in Oxford Street. This
the Duke could not stand; and he told the story in
every direction. It is to be hoped that in these
days of examinations such an awful solecism is now
totally unknown. I may say that notwithstanding
his ignorance of the humble art of etymology, the
individual in question played so successful a part in
life as anyone of his day.

THE DUKE invariably wore such uniform as he was
entitled to, that had relation to the circumstances in
which he was placed. On any Parade of the Guards
he invariably wore his dress as Colonel of the Grenadiers. The dress which, in my opinion, suited him best

was a Field Marshal's second dress; that is to say, with the plain blue collar and cuffs, no epaulettes, but a handsome double aiguillette on his right shoulder; a gold and red sash, with very handsome tassels, and the sword which I have described elsewhere with eagle head, which he wore when dismounted. When mounted he wore a curved scimitar. The sword given to him in India is represented in Count D'Orsay's spirited figure of him on horseback, now in the dining room at Apsley House.

I believe that considerable jealousy was harboured against him by the Duke of Cumberland, the latter a man, I cannot help believing, of sinister character; and although both were Tories of the severest school, I suspect they never were friends either politically or socially.

THE DUKE was most peremptory as regards each Regiment having distinctive marks: not only for sentiment, but far more, for practical purposes. As regards Regimental facings, and other distinctions, I am surprized that they should have been, to a great extent, abolished; and for this reason; it surely must be desirable that each Regiment should be distinguished, not by the enemy, but by the Officer commanding the Division, or Brigade. The enemy at a moderate distance cannot possibly tell the difference between blue and green, yellow and white; nor indeed observe the facing, so long as it is confined to the cuffs and collar; whereas the General Officer can discriminate at once; and order this or that Regiment to perform this or that duty.

As regards the colour red, I am surprized that it is not so much in favour now as it used to be; the belief that it offers a conspicuous mark to the enemy is, I should say, more or less delusive. The effect of weather upon red cloth, when exposed, is to render it very soon, as we all know, of a violet colour. Any fox-hunter's coat will testify to this. Again, the men's coats being, of course, of not of a brilliant scarlet, the colour is by no means conspicuous. In twilight red becomes invisible sooner than any colour. The Duke, in a dispatch from Spain, alludes to the proposal to alter the British uniform. He says emphatically "Whatever you do, our uniforms must not resemble those of any foreign country." He adds "It is absolutely necessary that I should be able to distinguish my Regiments of Infantry, Artillery, and Cavalry, from the enemy's," and he gives, as an illustration, that the unsightly and cruel short tails of the British

Dragoon Horse at that period, were an excellent
means of knowing his own Cavalry from that of the
enemy.

WILLIAM IV. was surely right, although it caused,
as I know, in the 7th and many other Regiments great
annoyance, when he said that all his soldiers should be
clothed in red; altering the pelisse, but not the jacket,
of the Hussars into scarlet.

A serious disaster befell a British Regiment of Infantry in consequence of the orders being given at
Quatre-Bras to deploy, notwithstanding the remonstrance of its Commanding Officer to his General that
the enemy's Cavalry was near. The reply he received
from the General, who was not a British subject, was
"You need have no anxiety; those are your own
Cavalry, wearing blue." In a very few minutes the
unfortunate Regiment was cut up by this very body of
cavalry.

Red has been hitherto the conquering colour:
surely it is worth while to retain this colour: at any
rate, so long as it retains this character.

WHEN GENERAL OUDINOT besieged Rome in
1849, he received the strictest injunctions not to

damage any Work of Art, architectural or other, within the walls. Someone pointing out to the Duke that General Oudinot was a very long time getting into the Eternal City, he replied "It is not very easy to break into a house, when you mustn't crack a window."

THE FACT that the Duke combined Honesty with Intellect was not to be endured. Cleverness being associated in the commonplace mind with the idea of Roguery, it must have been very exasperating to find a man combining transcendent Wit with absolute purity of purpose : no wonder that the Duke, whenever opportunity offered, was maligned.

I have said that the Duke was not a Beauty; but he possessed the highest quality, in looks, for a man : that of consummate Dignity : Grace being its counterpart in Woman. No one could look at the Duke and not see that he was a born gentleman : perfectly natural and simple in his manner; calm philosophic Thought, combined with unlimited Energy was shown in his face, and in his demeanour.

DISRAELI told me that the best reading he had ever had was the Middle Series of the Duke of Wellington's Dispatches ; from 1819 to 1832.

THE HISTORY of the Duke of Wellington's Sword
was told to me by the 2nd Duke at a dinner party at
Lady Elizabeth Steele's, 22 Upper Brook Street.
Some time afterwards the Duke, at Apsley House,
placed the Sword in my hands, saying "That is my
father's sword which I told you about." I have
lately examined it twice in the glass case in which it
lies at Apsley House. It is at present labelled "Sword
worn by the Duke of Wellington in the Peninsula."
It has a black scabbard with a very deep gilded cap
on the point with Eastern ornamentation ; two loops
for the "carriers"; no guard whatever over the gripe.
On returning to my chambers I examined the water-
colour portrait which I have of the Duke, by Dighton.
The Sword which the Duke wears in that portrait is
the same as that which I have just named. I also
took the opportunity of again examining in the supper-
room at Apsley House the silver-gilt statuette of the
Duke by Count d'Orsay. The same Sword is precisely copied in every detail in this Statuette. I may
point out also that in my water-colour by Dighton
the sword-knot hangs over the hand, and might be
taken for a "guard"; there is no "guard" whatever
to this sword, which is thoroughly Eastern in character.
Wishing to be perfectly accurate on such a very in-

teresting matter, I will add that the sword worn by the
Duke in the indifferent portrait of him with a cloak,
telescope etc., by Sir Thomas Lawrence, is a sword of
a different character. It is apparently French; but
might be of any nation. The mounting is brass; and
there is a slight bar as a guard for the hand. It is
curved, but of a completely different character from
the Eastern sword given to the Duke after Assaye.
Of this I am quite certain: that the Sword which I
have described as such was the actual sword presented
to the Duke after the battle of Assaye.

WHEN THE ALLIED ARMIES in their smart uniforms occupied Paris, the British soldiers appeared in
the dress in which they had fought the campaign.
This produced a great effect upon the French; and
upon impartial spectators.

A SOLDIER BELIEVES, and the belief ought to
be encouraged, that the character of his Regiment is
the one thing that he should esteem. Some may not
care much for their own character; and still less for
that of their family; nor for the Army of which they
form a part; but a real soldier, when appealed to in the
name of his Regiment, will always feel acutely if he
has disgraced it.

LORD ANGLESEY'S LEG was amputated at
Waterloo; in a house nearly opposite the Inn which
was then the head-quarters of the Duke. My father
was with him; and held his hand at the time of the
amputation.

THE ORIGIN of the flat watches, which have been
popular for several generations, is curious. When the
Allies took possession of Paris, there was, of course, a
great demand for French watches. "Breguet," and
"Le Roy" are names still famous. Up to that time
watches had been convex; in fact they acquired the
name of "turnips" from their shape. The reason of
the change of form was this. In several foreign
armies, particularly the Russian, smart Colonels
objected to the "bulbous" appearance of watches
either in the breast of the uniform, or the "fob" of the
nether garments; considering that they spoiled the
symmetry of the figure: hence came the necessity for
the watchmakers of the "Palais Royal" to contrive a
method of avoiding this difficulty; and we have since
had the blessing, no small one, of flat watches. Let
anyone compare his father's watch with his grandfather's; he will appreciate the change.

I have a flat watch given to my father by Lord

Anglesey very soon after Waterloo. It was bought of Le Roy in 1814, and has the Earl's Coronet of Uxbridge.

THE FATHER of my friend M. S., a North Devon Worthy, accompanied the Duke on his visit to Antwerp, after Waterloo. The Duke was received there, as elsewhere, by the multitude with wild enthusiasm. They clung round his horse; and used every expression of idolatry. The Duke took not the slightest notice: and when his companion asked him if he was pleased, he replied "Not in the least: if I had failed, they would have shot me."

WHEN THE EMPEROR NICHOLAS visited the Houses of Parliament, he called the building "Un rêve en pierre."

During the time that he was in England, one heard nothing but the Russian Hymn, a beautiful air arranged by his pianist Wolff: Haynes Bayly's Song "I'd be a Butterfly," played slowly.

I REMEMBER a conversation which took place at a dinner party at the Duke of Somerset's, the father of the present Duke, in Park Lane. There were several

" Heroes of Waterloo" there; among them Lord Strafford, formerly Sir John Byng, of Hougomont, and Sir James Kempt. They spoke of the march to Paris after Waterloo. Lord Strafford mentioned a remark made by a very distinguished General Officer on the road. After deploring the terrible loss of good soldiers among the officers and men, he added "And all this for a man who never was in love in his life."

No doubt it was to remove this terrible cause of offence in the eyes of the French people that Louis XVIII.'s Platonic intimacy with Madame Ducayla was instituted.

Several of the stories which I have related, I heard at the Duke of Somerset's hospitable board. His Duchess, a Scotch lady, loved to invite the great men of an earlier day. I may mention here a curious fact, which neither Lord Seymour nor his brother, the grandsons of the Duke I allude to, had ever heard. A small balcony placed on a level with the bedroom windows, at the angle of the house nearest to Oxford Street, was removed a few years ago. None of the family knew for what purpose that balcony was placed there. It not only faced the Park, but also was continued round the corner where there was no window.

The purpose for which this balcony was erected was to watch the executions at Tyburn Tree.

ON THE FIRST PAGE of this volume I have not alluded to the Prince of Orange. The Prince, holding the rank of full General, was nominally the Second in Command; but it cannot be supposed that the Duke would commit the destinies of Europe to an inexperienced lad of twenty-two.

The 1st Lord Seaton, who was the Prince's Military Secretary, but who acted with his Regiment the 52nd at Waterloo, Spoke of him as a "growing lad." Of exceptional bravery, when severely wounded, and carried from the field, he took off his principal decorations, and handed them to the Officers of the Regiment near which he fell. They still preserve them.

It has occurred to me, only as a possibility, that Lord Seaton, then Col. Colborne, being at his elbow, the Prince of Orange might have succeeded the Duke.

THE DUKE writing to a very intimate friend after Waterloo says "I never had so much trouble with a battle in my life"; speaking of it as a man would, I assume, of a domestic quarrel.

I have been told by two General Officers that they

heard the Duke say, speaking of Waterloo, "If I had
had my 'Bordeaux' army at Waterloo, I'd have swept
him off the face of the earth in two hours"; sweeping
his closed hand across the table.

IT WAS BY THE DUKE'S advice that the Queen's
Palace of Westminster, better known as the Houses
of Parliament, was built where it is. A far better
position, as regards centrality and convenience, might
have been chosen on or near the site of St James's
Palace. The Duke, however, gave advice to which
there could be no answer. He said, "With a vast
and growing population, such as yours in London, you
must never make it possible that you can be surrounded. You must build your House of Parliament
upon the river: so that the means of ingress and
egress are safe: and that the populace cannot exact
their demands by sitting down round you." I
mentioned this fact at an interesting interview which
I had with the Emperor Napoleon III. not long
before his death. He seemed a good deal struck
with the idea; and said twice "What Wisdom!
what Wisdom!" It doubtless occurred to him that
the history of France might have been different,
if a similar precaution had been taken.

SPEAKING ONE DAY to M[r] George Hudson, known as 'The Railway King,' a very shrewd York-shireman, I said that I never could understand why Lord Hardinge, though possessing ability, should have been placed in the very high position of Commander in Chief. M[r] Hudson replied: "The man, Sir William, whom the Duke of Wellington chose to be his second in a duel, is no ordinary man." This answer seemed to me at the time to be very good indeed: but on reflection, and reading, as I have done carefully, the circumstances of the Duke of Wellington's duel with Lord Winchilsea, I came to the conclusion that the Duke had selected Lord Hardinge because he was one who would do what he was told. The Duke, with his admirable shrewdness, felt that he had head enough for any number of men. The imputation made against the Duke was most unworthy; and it seems very much to be regretted that Lord Winchilsea did not absolutely and completely retract it. The Duke, as exceptional men do, knew clearly where Honour stops. He felt that the imputation made against him was not the ordinary imputation of one Statesman against another; but that it reflected upon his personal character. He had no doubt that he must, and ought to resent it. He gave his adversary every opportunity of retracting; and, according to what Lord Winchilsea's eldest son told me, fired straight at him, when on the field.

I BELIEVE THAT the Duke of Wellington as a boy, and young man, showed no marks of intellect. Like many men of surpassing energy, he probably found Latin grammar not to his taste. Indeed, I believe that in general the greatest minds mature latest; and are

"Mellowed by the stealing hours of Time."

THE ATTITUDE of the Duke, in Landseer's picture, showing the field of Waterloo to Lady Douro, makes him much too senile. On horseback, he never had that appearance in the least. Landseer evidently felt that he could not represent his face well, and has made him turn away from the spectator. I cannot believe that the Duke ever had a yellow stripe down his white trousers.

THE DUKE OF WELLINGTON in a letter which he wrote in French not long after the Battle of Waterloo, speaks of it as a "Battle of Giants": he used the

same term in a speech which he made in the House
of Lords on the subject of the Militia Bill; almost
the last speech, and a most excellent one, which
he ever delivered. He there said "Avowedly a
Battle of Giants."

THE DUKE'S EMOLUMENTS as Generalissimo
of the Allied Armies which occupied France after
Waterloo were enormous. It had been agreed that
these armies should remain for five years; and it was
by his own strenuous, and utterly disinterested exertions that the period was reduced to three. During
this time it was suggested that the French army should
be led against Italy by the Duke. He describes this
proposal as "all nonsense."

THE DUKE OF MARLBOROUGH was older at
his first battle than the Duke at his last.

WE DO NOT KNOW the Duke's views as regards
the prudence of sending Napoleon to Elba. One is
surprized indeed that such a risk should have been
run. As regards his return from Elba, the matter has
been imperfectly reasoned upon. It is clear that, had
Napoleon waited, the Powers assembled at Vienna

must have come to a coolness; if not a quarrel. The reason of Napoleon's apparently premature return was that his informants told him that the Family of Orleans were intriguing for the throne. That this was true is confirmed by the fact that on hearing that Napoleon had landed at Frèjus, Fouché, Duke of Otranto, the arch-intriguer, advised Louis XVI., previous to his leaving France, to make the Duke of Orleans Lieutenant-General of the Kingdom. This seems very like an attempt on the Throne, developed earlier than its projectors intended.

THE WORD "WELLINGTON" inscribed on the Waterloo Medal is, I should say, the only case of a man wearing a medal bearing his own name. The medal has not much pretension as a work of art; but is inoffensive. It is a curious illustration of the different extrinsic values which these things possess that it became necessary to make the Medal a "Soldier's Necessary"; so that he would be punished if he sold, or pawned it. I assume that it was made of silver, so that the soldier might attach more value to it : the secret of the preservation of these things is that the material of the article should be valueless; the extrinsic value priceless.

I ASSUME that to one in the position of the Duke whose every word would be valued and repeated, it was necessary to have a conventional courtesy of reply, which may or may not have touched his conscience. I remember perfectly at a Ball at Devonshire House, standing at the head of the white marble staircase when the Duke of Wellington walked up the stairs. He came late : I heard a lady say "I suppose, Duke, you have been to see the new play?" the occasion being, unless I am mistaken, the private performance of Lord Lytton's play "Not so bad as we seem," for the benefit of the "Guild of Literature and Art." The Duke replied "Yes, I have." "What did you think of it?" "Very good indeed; very good indeed. Capital, capital ; very good indeed." He then walked on into the crowd. A few minutes later I happened to be in the drawing-room. I heard another lady say "Tell me, Duke, what was the play about?" "Couldn't hear a word : not a word." This, I feel sure, like my Uncle Toby's oath, must have been blotted out by the Recording Angel.

AS REGARDS THE ENVY by which he was surrounded until the later years of his life, he, no doubt, took the practical view expressed by Sir Walter Scott.

Sir Walter compares one who has acquired Fame to him who gallops through a village : all the curs bark at him : he adds, with his usual good sense, that should he stop to chastise each, he would not reach the end of his journey. The Duke's coincided with this view.

I FOUND that Mr Knox, author of novels, who lived at Brighton, had purchased every newspaper published on the announcement of the Duke's death. Should my volume come into the hands of the present owner, I should be glad to purchase the collection.

I collected the leading articles of every European Newspaper on the announcement of the death of the Emperor Napoleon III.

THE DUKE was one of those men whom one cannot fancy laughing. He had a strong sense of humour ; like all men of clear intellect.

THE DUKE did everything that was possible to prevent plunder on the part of his troops in Spain : if he expressed himself with occasional bitterness about them, notwithstanding their courage, it can be accounted for by the extreme annoyance which this

conduct gave him. He was, however, just : he never
hesitated to praise those who, in this respect, followed his strict injunctions. He recognized the high
state of discipline in which were the Battalions of
Guards : and in several instances exempted them
from appearing on Parade, when an execution took
place, or even a reprimand was given by him to other
Regiments. In a General Order, dated Cartaxo, 3rd of
March, 1811, in which the finding and sentence of a
General Court-Martial on a soldier for desertion and
robbery is confirmed, and the sentence, that of being
hanged until dead, ordered to be carried into execution, in the presence of the troops at Cartaxo, in
order to deter others from the commission of similar
crimes, the following is the concluding paragraph :
"As during the two years during which the Brigade of
Guards has been under the command of the Commander of the Forces not only no soldier has been
brought to trial before a General Court Martial, but
no one has been confined in a public guard, the
Commander of the Forces desires that the attendance
of the Brigade of Guards at the execution to-morrow
may be dispensed with."

IN AN EARLIER PART of this work I told the

story of President Grant dining at Apsley House.
I regret that I asked the 2nd Duke what really took
place. However, as the reader has had the full enjoyment of the story, I must now, in the interests of
truth, state what the Duke told me happened. He
said that during dinner General Grant kept trying to
get him to say what was the greatest number of men
that his father had commanded in the field. The
Duke added "I saw what he was at; if I had said
forty or fifty thousand men, he would have replied,
'Well, I have commanded a hundred thousand;'
so I was determined not to answer his questions as
to this; and I succeeded."

WILLIAM IV. made an excellent change in the
dress of the army. He insisted upon the Officers of his
Regular Troops wearing Gold lace; of the Irregular,
Silver. It appears hard that a man who has gone
round the world, and devoted his life to serving in the
most unhealthy climates, and who has been repeatedly
in action, should wear the same uniform as one who
has never left his own County. As regards the enemy
being supposed to distinguish between the Militia
and Regular Regiments, the Militia Regiments have
always shown themselves to be quite equal to their

brethren in arms; indeed more than one of the battles in Spain was won mainly by men who had just joined from the Militia. The notion that, at a quarter of a mile, or indeed at a hundred yards, after a little bad weather, the enemy could distinguish between gold and silver lace seems ludicrous.

WHEN THE DUKE was asked about the new conical bullet, he said "Not less than an ounce; or it will not break a horse's leg;" meaning, of course, that the diameter should not be less than that of an ounce ball. This particular advice was not understood; nor followed.

IT HAS BEEN SAID that the words "Glorious," and "Glory," do not occur in the Duke's Dispatches. As a matter of historic truth, this is not the case. They do occur: but the Duke never appealed to them as an incentive to his soldiers.

AN INSTANCE of the Duke's shrewdness, and self-respect occurred at the opening of the great Exhibition of 1851. While waiting for Her Majesty to arrive, a Chinaman, in his native costume, walked into the inner circle of the Ministers, Court etc., and addressed the

Duke. The latter saw at a glance that the man was of no importance in his own country, beckoned to a policeman; and had him instantly removed.

THE CROWN has no longer the power to create Irish peers. When Disraeli was asked whether an Irish Peerage was valuable, I heard him say "Valuable! why the World is governed by Irish peers; look at Castlereagh, and Palmerston."

AT ONE TIME much nonsense was talked as regards the valueless character of "Prestige": Lord Russell sneered at it. The Duke had too much good sense to take such views. He knew that the dominant power of England, as proved in 1815, and the Prestige of his own name, preserved the Peace of Europe for forty years. He was the Keystone of European Peace. No sooner was he gone than difficulties began : and developed into a bloody, and more or less useless, War. Such was the opinion held of his Wisdom, and Honesty by European Statesmen that not one would dare to move seriously had he objected.

WELL MIGHT be applied to the Duke the words of the great Irish Orator in relation to Lord Chatham :

"The Secretary stood alone ; modern Degeneracy had not reached him."

Well might the Duke echo the words of Lord Chatham, "I live for the Wise and Good; the ignorant, and the malevolent I despise." [In a private note to Sir Edward Wilmot, his Physician.]

HORACE WALPOLE tells us that "Life is a Comedy to those who Think : a Tragedy to those who Feel." The Duke probably looked upon Life from the former point of view. His mind was healthy enough to be able to banish, after a time, Sorrow, and Suffering. It is impossible to conceive an Intellect such as his to have been devoid of Sensibility ; but the iron self-controul, which he invariably exercised, neutralized the effect of feeling. The Sense of Duty of a Wise Mind was the predominant, pervading characteristic of his nature.

ON THE OCCASION of a Reference being suggested to a young gentleman, whose conduct to a young lady had been compromising, the Arbitrators proposed were the Duke of Wellington, and Count d'Orsay. The selection was ingenious : it was not accepted.

SPEAKING TO LORD WINCHILSEA, son of the Duke's antagonist, he said "Everyone does not know that it was I who recited the Address to him at Oxford, when he was inaugurated in the Theatre." He added "I did not write the Address; and I forget the man's name who wrote it." I said "How I envy you that splendid Apostrophe; turning to the Duke unexpectedly, and saying

"And the stern soul the World could scarce subdue Bowed to thy Genius, CHIEF OF WATERLOO!"

I have ascertained subsequently, that though Lord Winchilsea did recite a Congratulatory Address to the Duke on that occasion, it was not his fate to declaim these lines. I have lately received from Sir J. M., a graphic account of the scene. The ordinary Prize Poem, usually known as "The Newdigate," was on the subject of "The Hospice of Mount St. Bernard": and this, of course, gave an opportunity for describing Napoleon's traversing the mountain : but the Apostrophe above quoted was unexpected; and the effect was electrical. The Undergraduates rose from their places and burst into one roar of applause. This was continued for several minutes. Then a pause : during which, on the Duke's motion, the Poet endeavoured to continue his recitation ; but the Undergraduates again rose ; and it seemed as if there would never be an end to their cheering. It must have been one of those moments never to be forgotten. The Duke sat perfectly unmoved.

THE DUKE, as is well known, stumbled over his "quantities." When he became Chancellor of Oxford, a quotation from Shakespeare was appropriate ;

"Never was such a sudden scholar made" :

and I suspect that during his Eton career he did not trouble his head much about Latin verse. Having pronounced the word "Jacŏbus" short, no doubt having heard the term Jacobite, and Jacobin used, he was corrected ; and immediately afterwards made another blunder, making the "o" in Carŏlus long. This must have excited considerable merriment in a Theatre full of Scholars. He made an excellent Chancellor ; and no one could have looked better in the Cancellarial robes.

THE DUKE seems to have had an indifferent opinion of Kings in general ; and certainly had no overweening appreciation of Louis XVIII. The latter, I believe, had no over-cordial feeling towards the Duke.

The Bourbons showed themselves a spoiled race : and I suspect that this was the case on their return. Louis XVIII. was undoubtedly the cleverest of his family; indeed he was a man of exceptional gifts. One trait of his Wisdom was exhibited on his death-bed. When informed by his Physicians that he could not live beyond a few days, the King at once sent for his Ministers; and said to them, "I shall be dead within a week. At once reduce the five per cents.: and shackle the Press. The hatred of the middle classes (la haine bourgeoise) will be buried in my coffin. Omit to do this, and it will cost my successor his throne." His orders were not obeyed : and we know the result.

WHEN THE DUKE was asked to what characteristic of his mind he attributed his invariable success, he replied "I attribute it entirely to the application of good sense to the circumstances of the moment."

THE DUKE, when in Spain, wisely allowed his Regimental Officers of all ranks to ride. Twaddle, of course, would denounce this, as setting a bad example to the men ; and say that the Officers avoided fatigues, which the men were obliged to submit to. The Officers showed themselves, when necessary, quite capable of sharing the hardships of the men : in fact it was not unfrequent for an Officer to lend his horse to a wounded, or fatigued man : the Duke considered that the balance was in favour of their riding ; and for this reason ; when the Regiment arrived with the men exhausted, if the Officers had been in the same condition, but little trouble would have been taken to provide for the night : whereas the Regimental Officers being comparatively fresh, they were enabled to assist, and stimulate the men, in making themselves what was ironically termed " comfortable for the night."

AS REGARDS political promotion, Lord Palmerston took a thoroughly sound view. On giving an Irish Member of Parliament (one P. S.) some small appointment, a critic remarked that the Member in question had not been sober for years. " Drunk, or sober," said Lord Palmerston, "I observe that he never mistakes our lobby."

THE DUKE had no very high opinion of an over-educated Officer ; that is to say one who relied upon

scientific knowledge, without having the good sense
to apply it instantly to circumstances. On one occasion
an officer was sent out to him whose reputation for
Military Science was very great. The Duke wrote
back " You have sent me A. B. He is as much fit to
be Adjutant-General of this army, as I am to be King
of England. I have always got on very well with
C. D." An Oxford graduate was his favourite type.

THE DUKE, when Prime Minister, organized a
system by which he could travel rapidly between
Strathfieldsaye, and Apsley House ; which, I believe,
is called in India "a Dauk." He purchased a
·Curricle; and he arranged for frequent relays of
post-horses along the road ; probably the most rapid
means of conveyance that could be contrived in those
days.

THE DUKE OF WELLINGTON AND CRAU-
FURD did not agree particularly well. Both were
men of exceptional capacity : and the Duke knew that
Craufurd was, what was sadly wanting in the British
army, a Scientific Soldier. He had been thoroughly
educated in his profession; in. addition to having

great intellectual power.   But he was hot-tempered :
and self-willed.

The first quality, I believe, the Duke did not
mind; but, knowing his own surpassing Wisdom, he
felt acutely being thwarted by those beneath him.   I
do not feel competent to criticise Craufurd's conduct
in relation to the battle of the Coa ; and, being
his nephew, I shall not presume to do so.   His
reception by the Duke the following morning on
Parade is well known.   "I am glad to see you safe
General Craufurd!" "I was never in danger." "Oh !
I was."   General Craufurd, walking away, said " He's
damned crusty this morning !" The Duke no doubt
felt that he must do one of two things, either send
General Craufurd to England ; or, if he could not
spare him, which no doubt was the case, to do nothing.
He adopted the latter course. The simple instructions
to storm Ciudad Rodrigo were carried out with the
greatest possible skill ; and General Craufurd lost his
life by placing himself in a position to see that everything was done with precise accuracy. He died when
in front, to the left, not only of the Storming Party,
but of the Forlorn Hope.

The Duke visited him on his death-bed ; and
Craufurd having expressed his deep regret that there

should have been a difference between them, the Duke subsequently related the conversation, saying "Craufurd talked to me as they do in a novel." The Duke and the whole of the Staff attended General Craufurd's funeral. One of the most striking pictures I have ever seen was shown many years ago at the Gallery of Illustration. Among a series of dissolving views was one of the Duke standing alone before the High Altar, in the Cathedral of Ciudad Rodrigo, looking at the coffin of General Craufurd, which was placed on a bier immediately in front of it.

I regret very much that I did not follow up an enquiry as to further minute particulars relating to the storming of Ciudad Rodrigo. My dear, and excellent friend, the 1st Lord Seaton, who commanded the 52nd on that night, could, I have no doubt, have told me much; and on one occasion, when staying at the Baierischer Hof at Munich, I sat next to Sir George Napier at the table d'hôte; and I cannot bear to think how much I might have learned from him. He lost an arm on that night, and could, doubtless, have given me numerous and valuable details. I may, however, say more on the subject another time. Sir James Shaw Kennedy, General Craufurd's A.D.C., wrote me a most clear and in-

teresting account of his General's death. General
Craufurd was buried in the breach which he had
taken ; and the bastion bears the name of " Craufurd's
Bastion."

I wish to place a tablet to my uncle's memory
in the Cathedral ; but his not being a member of the
Church of Rome may prevent my doing this.

LORD HILL was supposed to have had the Duke's
confidence more than any other General. He was
not, I believe, a man of very great abilities ; but had
one great merit in the eyes of the Duke : who said
" Hill does what he is told."

I remember my father saying this of him ; and it
has been said by others.

THE DUKE'S handwriting is indistinct. It is the
handwriting of a man who has written a great deal :
in fact he was always writing. One would be curious
to know what the verdict of those who read Character
from handwriting would be.

FROM THE TONE of the Duke's writings and
sayings it would seem as if even his splendid career
had not afforded him any supreme satisfaction. The

consciousness of having done his duty no doubt consoled him. It seemed hardly to have done more.
He must have felt in rising in the world the sensation
attributed to those who go up in a balloon. They
do not seem to rise : but the earth seems to sink :
as he got higher and higher in the atmosphere of
success, I should say the feeling I have described
must have prevailed in his mind.

A STORY IS TOLD of Lord William Lennox, when
serving in 'The Blues,' which may or may not be well
founded. The Cavalry Regiment at Windsor, in those
days, was paraded for Review at the back of the
Cavalry barracks, in meadows now partly built over.
Sir Charles Dalbiac, the Inspector-General of Cavalry,
on retiring with the Commanding Officer to luncheon,
desired that one of the Captains should put the Regiment through some simple movements in his absence.
Lord William Lennox was selected for this honour;
and before the end of the half hour, when the General
etc., returned, had succeeded, to use a technical term,
in 'clubbing' the Troops, and even the Sections,
effectually. At this critical moment Sir Charles
Dalbiac and his Staff reappeared at a distance. Lord
William showed himself not wanting in military judg-

ment. Looking at the conglomerate mass of the Regiment, which was a complete ' olla podrida,' he said, loud enough for the men to hear, and not loud enough for the General, " Royal Horse Guards ! Damn your eyes ! Find your places ! March !" A movement, indistinct in the distance, took place ; and by the time the Inspecting-General arrived ' The Blues ' were in perfect order.

IT HAS BEEN WISELY SAID that the man who excels in one thing alienates half mankind ; that he who excels in two has not a friend left. That the Duke should be honourable, and successful, was too much for his fellow creatures to endure. Had he been successful, and a rogue, well and good ; or had he been a highminded man, and failed, it might have been pardoned. The good, old, pagan saying that " the Gods are jealous of an honest man " is so true now as when Jupiter, and Juno ruled the roost ; and looked down laughingly upon the monkey tricks of mankind.

IT HAS BEEN ASKED, with some point, what possible firing could the Duke of Brunswick have heard when seated in the "long low room," which Byron idealises.

So far as History records, there was no firing whatever on the night between the 15th and 16th of June;

"The car rattling in the stony street,"

may have suggested the idea to his imagination; but as the French army was at Charleroi; and they had no one to fire at (there had been fighting in the day), this seems to be purely fanciful. It was very remarkable, that although the firing at Waterloo was heard in Norfolk, it was not heard by the Division of the Army that was out of sight of the field towards the west. They knew nothing till the next morning.

WATERLOO GAVE A PATENT of Nobility to all who were present. So long as Britain shall exist, a man who can trace his ancestry to one who fought at Waterloo, will have a position of distinction.

PROBABLY the most popular caricatures that came out in relation to the Duke were the set by Heath in which the Duke figures as the man "Wot drives the Sovereign." Another is "The Guard wot looks after the Sovereign." The Guard (Lady C.) is made to say to the King, "Keep your eye on them leaders, George."

WHEN LORD ANGLESEY was appointed to command the Cavalry for the Campaign of 1815, some one who was intimate with the Duke remarked to him that he thought Lord Anglesey's appointment would cause considerable scandal in London. The Duke asked why. "Your Grace cannot have forgotten the affair with Lady Charlotte." "Oh no ! I have not forgotten that." "That is not the only case, I am afraid. At any rate Lord Uxbridge has the reputation of running away with everybody he can." The Duke calmly replied, " I'll take good care he don't run away with me : I don't care about anybody else." In this anecdote I have been compelled to soften the vigorous vernacular of the Great Duke.

THE PRESENTATION of a flag on the morning of the anniversaries of the great battles of Blenheim and Waterloo is the tenure by which Blenheim, and Strathfieldsaye are held. The small, silk, gold-fringed flags are placed in Windsor Castle. I enquired at the shop in St James's Street which supplied them, as to what precautions were taken to ensure the delivery of the flag upon the proper days of each year, before noon. I learnt that a man was sent with the flag by an early train in the morning: that another was kept ready in case of accident. The Duke of Marlborough's is a white banner with three gold fleur de lis. The Duke's flag for Strathfieldsaye is a tricolour. After Waterloo the Duke was allowed to add to his Coat of Arms an 'Escutcheon of Pretence,' bearing the Field, Colours, and Crosses of the 'Union' flag.

IT HAS BEEN SAID that Ridicule is the test of the Sublime: it never seems to have had the slightest effect on the reputation of the Duke. The thousands upon thousands of caricatures which were issued for days, weeks, months, and years, did not diminish the respect in which he was held by the several generations in which he lived.

IN COMPARING the opportunities of the Duke and of Napoleon the First, people seem to forget what utterly different positions they held.

The Duke was under strict orders from home:

and had, when in Spain, very little controul over the political intentions of the Government.

His place was to obey their orders; and to do his best in circumstances frequently very difficult.

He had little means of knowing what was passing in the East of Europe.

He took his instructions from home : and as regards Foreign political matters, he must have been in the dark; or at any rate dependent entirely upon what the Government chose to tell him. He could no more order a conscription, nor levy troops ad libitum, than he could fly. He had to put up with the soldiers sent him from England; some of whom were, no doubt, a very bad lot; and he was bound to make the best of often very indifferent materials.

How completely different was the position of the Emperor Napoleon. The Autocrat of France : holding the wires, by which the mechanism was worked, in his hands alone; perfect master of his own secrets : well able to extort from the French Nation any number of soldiers : the destiny of those soldiers being entirely dependent upon his will, or caprice, his powers were enormously greater than those the Duke of Wellington ever had.

The more we read the history of the two men the

more marvellous do the Duke's exploits seem. To
sweep the Armies of France before him, out of a
difficult, and mountainous country like Spain ; to pass
from Victory to Victory ; and finally to lead his conquering army into the country of the enemy ; an
enemy grown desperate at last ; fills one with boundless admiration.

THE DUKE did ample justice to the brilliant
courage of the French at Waterloo ; and to the skill
with which the battle was conducted on their side.
He modestly says that he has repeatedly stated this,
not for his own glorification, but with the honest
conviction that it was impossible for troops to do
more than the French did. This no doubt was
the case. Justice has hardly been done to them by
their own writers. To the French people Success is
an essential for Praise: and whether it be their
Emperor losing his throne at Sedan, or a poor
soldier who bleeds to death in a ditch, scanty praise
is given by that race to Failure.

THE EXPECTED Commander of the Cavalry at
Waterloo was Lord Combermere : the Prince Regent

appointed Lord Anglesey. Lord Combermere was
esteemed the best Commander of Cavalry in Europe.

One small incident in Lord Combermere's life must
have gratified him. At the time when Civilians first
came to the conclusion that they knew a great deal
more about army matters than Soldiers, one of the
most conspicuous of them wrote to Lord Combermere
telling him that he, the writer, who held high office,
considered that the Standing Orders of the 1st Regiment of Life Guards, that is the Regulations that
controul the interior economy of a Regiment, Officers'
duties, etc., were unsuitable; and should be changed.
The writer also especially called Lord Combermere's
attention to the Standing Orders of the —th Regiment
of Cavalry of the line : and added that he thought
these latter might be adopted as a good model by
which a Regiment of Horse ought to be ruled.

Lord Combermere replied seriatim to the objections
to the Standing Orders of the 1st Life Guards of
which he was Colonel. He then added : " I have had
the honour to examine the Standing Orders of the
—th Regiment of Cavalry to which you have called
my attention. I read them not only with attention,
but with interest ; for they were written entirely by
myself, when I commanded that Regiment. I consider

them utterly, and totally unfitted for the 1ˢᵗ Regiment of Life Guards, whose Colonel I have now the honour to be."

OF ALL THE BLOWS struck of late years at the British Army none was felt more severely than that of taking away the Numbers of Regiments: a more wanton affront never was put upon any set of men: and nothing was ever felt more deeply.

It may of course be said, as it has been said, that the Numbers of Regiments were changed in the last century; and that many Battalions were embodied, dis-embodied, and re-embodied. All this is true; but it is a poor excuse.

The Classic Time of the British Army began with Egypt; and ended with Waterloo.

This period stands absolutely apart. Their glorious achievements, and the splendid renown that the British Regiments acquired during those eventful years can never be forgotten. Its recollection in the minds of soldiers should have been preserved by every possible means. Every distinction, whether by badges, facings, names of Battles on Colours, should have been carefully preserved. Almost every Regiment engaged in that great struggle won some special distinction: and no one who knows anything of a soldier's heart does not believe that he treasures these Emblems of Tradition above everything.

It would be invidious to recapitulate here the particular honours conferred, and the Numbers of particular Regiments who have won immortal glory. It was a cruel act to take them away : and an absurd one to place the names of Battles on the Colours of a·Regiment, which was not present as a Regiment, at the action named.

Nothing would be more popular, nor more wise, than the restoration of Numbers to the respective Regiments.

It is said that, by naming Regiments after Counties, and sections of Counties, what the French call an "Esprit du Clocher" will grow up. It may in time : but it will take another War of fifteen years, and a successful War, to give the Regiments a prestige equal to that of 1800-1815.

THE DUKE particularly disliked to be treated, spoken to, and of, merely as a Soldier. He always resented this. I should say, that he would have wished to be esteemed, as he was, a very great

Diplomatist. His perfect Honesty; and the conviction which the chief Diplomatists of Europe held
of that rare quality, served him in excellent stead.
No doubt he and Lord Castlereagh were England's
Great Men in those days. The latter has not been
done justice to: the Duke always had a very high
opinion of him. So superlative was the good sense
of the Duke, that he triumphed over the chicanery
of others. They might well say

> " His Nobleness of Spirit
> O'ertops our Genius."

His powerful mind did not stoop to the paltry
manœuvres of smaller beings. He acted on broad,
and noble principles; and scorned the miserable
tricks used by inferiors. He lived long enough to
prove to the world his complete disinterestedness;
and the marvellous acuteness of his intellect. These
two qualities, rare in combination, brought about his
final triumph. A French Statesman of long experience, hearing some disparaging remarks as to the
Duke's Simplicity in Diplomacy, said " Je connais le
Duc de Wellington: c'est un Diplomate fort à
craindre : il voit tres clairement son but ; et y marche
bien droitement." The breath had scarcely left his

body when the Eastern intrigue began. No one can doubt that had he lived the movement on the part of Russia would not have taken place; the Duke would have seen at once its object; his personal remonstrance would have checked it; or his splendid prowess would have defeated it.

I HAPPENED to be staying at the Castle in Dublin when the 33rd Regiment, which had just received the great distinction of bearing the name of "The Duke of Wellington's Own," was presented with its new Colours. I have never longed so much for the opportunity of making a speech as on that occasion. General D., who had just been made Colonel in Chief, addressed a very smart Regiment, principally composed of well set up young men. The Colours, presented by the wife of the Lord Lieutenant, bore the Duke's arms, and his grand family motto

"Virtutis Fortuna Comes."

Even an allusion to his greatness would have been something. Instead of this the poor old gentleman could find nothing better than to say that "the Duke was always a sober man." I am not sure that he did not add that the Duke did not smoke. The whole

exhibition was dull, and disgraceful. I believe he
managed to say, that where those Colours were brave
hearts would be gathered; which he had probably
read in a book. The next year in storming the
heights of the Alma this fine Regiment showed that
they were of the right sort; notwithstanding the
feeble address of the General, who was their Colonel
in Chief.

ON THE OCCASION of the Bill of Pains and
Penalties against Queen Caroline a good deal of
rioting took place on the road to the House of
Lords. The 3rd Lord Londonderry being surrounded
by a mob, who insisted on his crying "God Save
the Queen," took off his hat; and exclaimed "God
save Her Majesty; and may every one of you have
a wife like her."

Lord Brougham stated privately that he had no
doubt that Queen Caroline's mind was more or less
affected; and that this affection took the form of an
inordinate wish to nurse infants : whenever she saw
a mother, or nurse with a child in arms, she would
order it to be brought to her house at Blackheath.
This of course gave rise to the scandals, which at that
time surrounded her. As regards the parentage of

William Austin there could be no doubt that his
father and mother were clearly identified by the
Government; and although prudence dictated this
step, the result was thoroughly satisfactory.

IT HAS BEEN SAID as a good illustration of the
difficulty of ascertaining facts that when the Duke at
a great Review in Hyde Park, where many thousands
of persons were looking on, fell from his horse, no
agreement could be found as to what had happened.
Some said the horse reared; others that he 'bucked.'
Some that he laid down, and rolled upon the Duke;
others that the Duke had a fit; some said that it was
in going away; others that it was soon after arriving.
No one agreed as to where the fall occurred: a
large number declared that he had no fall at all.

SOON AFTER the Duke's death, Roebuck, the
Member for Sheffield, told a story in a speech at
that place, which he subsequently assured me was
precisely true. Staying in a country house, he heard
the news of the Duke's death. He spoke, in the early
morning, to the gardener, an elderly man, who was
mowing the lawn. He said: "There is bad news
come." "Is there, sir?" said the man. "Yes," he

said; "the Duke's dead at last." "Who sir?"
"The Duke of Wellington." "I'm very sorry for
the gentleman," replied the man, going on with his
work; "but I never heard of him."

WALKING WITH DISRAELI, he told me the
following story. I have never made up my mind
whether he believed it to be true or not. He spoke
as if he implicitly believed it.

Speaking of the small circle in which even the
greatest move, he told me that the First Napoleon,
a year after he became Emperor, was determined to
find out if there was anyone in the world who had
not heard of him. Within a fortnight the Police of
Paris had discovered a wood-chopper at Montmartre,
within Paris, who had never heard of the Revolution;
nor the death of Louis XVIth; nor of the Emperor.

BRUSSELS during the Campaign of Waterloo has
been painted in deathless colours by Thackeray. He
asked me which I thought to be the best passage
of all his writings: I said; "No more firing was
heard. The pursuit rolled miles away. Darkness
came down on the Field; and on the City: and

Amelia was praying for George; who was lying on his face; dead; with a bullet through his heart."

I was riding past Stafford House, when I met Swinton, the Painter. He told me of Thackeray's death. On entering Hyde Park I saw Alfred Wigan, the Actor, and told him the news. We went together at once to Thackeray's house in Kensington; I have narrated in verse the circumstance that occurred:

W. M. T.

The fog is dank in Rotten Row;
 The Sun a disc of dingy red:
" How are you?" " How d'ye do?" "No news
 Is there?" " Yes; Thackeray is dead."
A breathless gallop to his door:
 The footman for a moment pales;
" They're searching for the cause of death
 Upstairs: *I've taken up the Scales.*"

Ironic Fate! fell Humour thine!
 The Brain but yesterday that glowed
And glittered in the air of Wit
 Has left its fifty years' abode:

A World his penstrokes watched yestreen ;
  Last night a film of tissue fails :
" How many ounces weighs his brain ? "
  And then ; " *I've taken up the Scales.*"

Oh deeply-cutting Workman dead !
  Oh mighty Mind gone from our gaze !
Oh child-like Heart ! oh, priest of Truth !
  Sky-piercing marble let us raise !
Oh judgment-giving King ! while Truth
  To poise the rolling World avails,
Say from thy tomb, " With giant's grasp,
  Of Men *I've taken up the Scales.*"

When, millions of dead Æons gone,
  Thy Glorious Spirit shall arise :
And listen to the thunder-peals :
  And watch the lightnings of the skies :
Then, when the Spheres their Music cease ;
  While Silence o'er all Space prevails ;
Hear, undismayed, the Eternal Voice
  Pronounce, " I'VE TAKEN UP THE SCALES ! "

NO MILITARY SPECTACLE of the kind, that I have seen, has equalled that of the Duke's coming on to the Parade of the Flank Companies of the Foot Guards, in the rear of the Horse Guards, on the morning of the Queen's birthday. The Duke, as Commander in Chief, accompanied by a numerous, and most splendid Staff, rode down Constitution Hill from Apsley House. He was dressed in the uniform of his Regiment, the Grenadier Guards. The line was of course formed previous to his arrival; with the squadron of the Life Guards on duty on the right flank.

At the first stroke of the Horse Guards' clock, the Duke appeared on the left flank of the line. At the moment that his horse passed the extreme left, the word was given by the Commanding Officer to stand at "Attention"; then "Present arms": instantly the magnificent band of the three Regiments of Guards, with their drums and fifes, numbering together over 200 instruments, played the first note of Handel's glorious air. Not since the composition of "See the Conquering Hero comes" can it ever have been given under more effective circumstances. While listening to that grand melody, you looked at the mighty Conqueror.

The Duke, on arms being presented, instantly and slowly raised his right hand, nearly touching the lower right edge of his bearskin with two fingers. He rode slowly across the Parade; and the ceremony of "Trooping the Colours" was gone through. During this time some well chosen air, not unfrequently the "Benediction des Poignards," from "Les Huguenots," was played. The March-Past followed. The united bands played Mozart's noble melody "Non piu andrai"; the finest march for slow time that ever was composed. Afterwards the Guards marched past in quick time; the Grenadiers playing "The British Grenadiers"; the Coldstream Guards a beautiful March known as "The Milanollo," the most perfect, as regards time, that I have heard. The Scots Guards, the national, but mediocre melody "Will ye go to Inverness?" The line then advanced; and presented arms; the Duke again saluted: leaving the ground amidst tumultuous cheering.

THE DUKE OF WELLINGTON speaking of Napoleon frequently called him "Jonathan Wild the Great," a humorous expression which will be understood by those who have read the life of the latter by De Foe. He seems to have had a much more just

appreciation of Napoleon than Napoleon had of him.
Nothing could be more absurd than the Emperor's
idea expressed at St Helena, that the Duke of
Wellington would, or could take possession of the
Throne of England. The first Napoleon's downfall
was mainly owing to his utter incapability of com-
prehending the British Character. He took a conventional and vulgar view of Mankind; and was
utterly baffled by those who have shown themselves
to be unconventional. The Irish Poet understood
the British when he said they were

"With daring aims; Irregularly Great."

WHITE'S IS NOW A CLUB: it was an Institution: an Institution of the most powerful, and
effective character, which for 130 years ruled the
Society of London as regards men, with wonderful
discrimination, and marvellous force. To be admitted a member of that body gave a young man a
"cachet" such as nothing else could give. Looking
through the volumes of candidates for many years,
the discrimination to be observed is marvellous.
The absolute qualifications are difficult to define;
but still are strongly marked. "Je ne sçais quoi" its
device. Neither Rank, Wealth, Wit, nor any quality

in itself, enabled a candidate to be sure of election : and although the blackballing, which in some instances continued for years, appears at first tyrannical, it rarely happened that ultimately the individual, if possessing the particular qualifications desired, did not gain admission. Some were excluded, notwithstanding the annual efforts of a lifetime : some few were admitted at once : but, sooner or later, Justice was done.

The Duke had a high opinion of that mysterious and terrible tribunal "White's Bow Window." Disraeli describes it in "Lothair" as being occupied by a few cynical middle-aged gentlemen, from whose presence "Lothair," after reading a newspaper upside down, retires. In the days I speak of no man under forty ever ventured to sit within that sacred semicircle : and there was more shrewdness, good sense, and knowledge of things, to be found there than in any other space of the same size on the surface of the Globe.

I remember before the Franco-German War was begun, one member, sitting there, asking another "What is this to be?" The reply was, "A race to Bavaria." This turned out to be absolutely true : for, had the French succeeded in reaching Munich,

there can be no doubt that the Bavarians, and South
Germans, would have taken up their cause. Before
the last war between Russia and Turkey, I remember
the question being put there: "What do the Russians
want?" the answer was: "Bessarabia, and Batoum":
precisely what they obtained.

NO GREATER INSTANCE of the Duke's quick-
ness could be found than his rapid coup d'œil when
he rode to St Sebastian. He pointed out at once that
the attack was being made from the wrong stand-
point; and by his directions, the troops attacking
crossed the river at low water, and stormed the
breach successfully. My old friend, the Duke of
Saldanha, commanded a Brigade during the attack.
He told me that one evening when he was wash-
ing his hands for dinner a shot came, knocking the
basin to atoms; without however even touching his
fingers. The popular idea of a Portuguese General is
that he should have a dark, sallow, and rather worn
countenance; the Duke of Saldanha was the most
refined type of John Bull that I have ever seen;
clear blue eyes, bright complexion, a look of extreme
intelligence, and with a polished bluffness that was
very charming. I saw him in his coffin; and in-

stead of being past eighty, his appearance was as that
of a man of forty; and his face almost the handsomest
that I have seen.

THE DUKE said that he had obtained a hint from
Lord Anglesey in relation to Cavalry crossing a river
that was the most valuable on the subject that he had
heard from anyone. Lord Anglesey told him that for
certain reasons, which I cannot here more exactly
describe, no Cavalry could exist, if the water were
above the horses' backs, for more than three quarters
of an hour. The Duke said that he found this knowledge most useful when crossing the rivers into France.

THE DUKE'S OPINION of the French Marshals
was not very high. No doubt Napoleon was afraid
to give a man command who had superior military
knowledge: in case of a defeat by himself the other
might have become a dangerous rival. The Duke,
with the good nature that always marked his conduct,
avoided individual criticism of his opponents. He
knew that his word would be carried: and knew how
difficult it is to form a just opinion of one to whom
you are opposed. Walking with a friend in Paris in
1815, and passing a statue which was in process of

erection, the friend remarked, that after all, although the French had been ultimately defeated, it was a grand thing to be able to put up so many statues to their Generals. The Duke quietly said, "Yes; and if they knew as much about them as I do, they'd take down a good many." Massena (Manasseh) was, in the opinion of the Duke, and of Napoleon, the best in action.

I HAVE ALWAYS HAD a fixed opinion as regards the death of Desaix : and have little doubt by whose hand he fell. The death of Pichegru, murdered in his prison ; and of the Duke d'Enghien in the ditch at Vincennes, the same man being close at hand in each case, confirm my theory.

HOW STRANGE it is that Napoleon, the great conqueror, entirely failed in attaching the affections, so far as fidelity was in the case, of either of his wives.

LORD SEATON, by whose friendship I was honoured up to the time of his death, was certainly the noblest type of a soldier that I have known.

He told me, I remember, when I was on his Staff at Chobham, that the hill opposite our lines, crowned with pine trees, was not unlike the heights of Busaco. I cannot help dwelling for a moment upon his character. Mildest, kindest, gentlest of human beings; clear-headed, calm, vigorous in mind as he was strong in body, he was always my idea of a Soldier. In speaking to him you felt that the good, unworldly being you were talking to was the same gallant spirit who had headed the 52nd at Ciudad Rodrigo; and had taken part in all the desperate actions in which that heroic body fought. He had not much graphic power of description; indeed very few men have; but I regret that I did not ask him more questions in relation to the Peninsular War. He was well known to, and thoroughly trusted by, the Duke.

I HAVE READ a very interesting letter addressed to my uncle General Robert Craufurd by The Right Hon. William Windham. It was written not long before the unfortunate expedition to Walcheren. He says in it that the Expedition will be the most perfect, as regards arrangements and organization, that has ever left England. He expresses regret that it is not to be sent to the Peninsula, nor to be placed under the orders of the Duke, of whom he adds "I begin to think that your chief (the Duke) has some military

ability." M' Windham at the end of this letter says
that no expedition however well organized, and however well fitted for conquest, can ever succeed "if
placed under the command of such a man as the Earl
of Chatham." We know the terrible disaster that followed; owing almost entirely to the want of good
sense in the British Government at home. The fate
of Europe would have been changed, had those
30,000 men been sent to Spain.

Due political appreciation has hardly been given to
the great effects of the Duke's success in the Peninsula: the overwhelming loss of the French Army in
the premature snows of Russia, for the season was
early, has distracted historical attention from what
took place in 1812 in Spain. Napoleon's mind never
was at ease from the moment when he saw the beginning of British success: the defeat of his Armies
in succession in Spain was the "ver rongeur" that dis-
turbed his rest. However much he may have affected,
for a purpose, to sneer at the British troops, his
military perception was too astute not to be early convinced that they were, and would prove themselves
still more to be, dangerous customers.

I DO NOT KNOW whether the Duke had anything

to say to the appointment of Sir Hudson Lowe to be the custodian of Napoleon at St Helena; but it was no doubt an unfortunate selection. My father used to say that Sir Hudson, though not a bad soldier, was wanting in many of the essentials of a Gentleman. No doubt it must have been very difficult to find a man with the rare combination of 'suaviter in modo' with 'fortiter in re,' who would undertake such heavy responsibility, involving banishment from his own country; and accept an office which every sensible man would know was sure to lead to abuse, and calumny. Still the appointment seems to have been made somewhat hurriedly: and it certainly turned out ill. It gave Napoleon a sort of justification for some of his usually unfounded complaints.

The cause of Napoleon's decline of hope, and with it his decline of health, was the fact that Lord Holland's motion in the House of Lords in his favour had no seconder.

Knowing as he did the absolute independence of the Members of that House of Parliament, he must have felt that if there were not two Peers to support his cause it was indeed desperate.

MADAME CRAUFURD, at whose house the Duke was a constant guest in Paris, was an Irish woman by birth; extraordinarily handsome, and clever, she was for many years almost at the head of the fashionable world in Paris; a somewhat surprizing circumstance, considering her not very distinguished origin. She lived in the Rue d'Anjou. Mr Quentin Craufurd had behaved with exceptional loyalty to the Royal House of France. It was he who provided the carriage which conveyed Louis XVIth, Marie Antoinette, and their family to Varennes. Owing to two circumstances, the Dauphin refusing to be dressed as a girl, and the cavalry picket being placed at the wrong end of the town, the unfortunate family was captured. As they drove back through Paris, someone in the crowd said, "I know that carriage: it is Craufurd's." A friend, fortunately standing by, adroitly replied, "Oh, no, it is not: I know his carriage very well." No more pathetic sight could be seen than the poor children of the King, who had been taught to kiss their hands in reply to the cheers of the multitude, still doing so, while the foul wretches who surrounded the carriage were thirsting for their blood.

On learning the news that the King and Queen had

been captured, Mʳ Quentin Craufurd, who was in safety at Brussels, immediately returned to Paris, and had a most interesting interview with Marie Antoinette, at the Tuileries.

The Queen asked for his ring, as a means of communicating with him. Mʳ Craufurd expressing hope, with reference to the engraving on it, a bird holding a branch, the Queen replied, "No, I have no hope for myself. My one prayer is, that my son may reign."

AS REGARDS George IV. towards the end of his life much nonsense was talked. The late Lord Lucan, with whom I had several conversations on the subject, and who at the period was in London Society, told me that anything so ridiculous, as the notion of the multitude relating to George IV. could not be conceived. As for the two old ladies with whom as Prince Regent, and King, he associated, one, Lady H., was exceptionally ugly; and his last innamorata, Lady C., preposterously fat. The King liked gossip; was soon weary of his own company: and these two old ladies furnished him with a daily pabulum of news: either he believed that his visits to Hamilton Place were unknown; or, more probably, was quite indifferent whether they were known or not. The elderly person supposed to be the object of the King's attachment was glad no doubt to 'pavoner' herself; and to excite the envy of her Sex by his exceptional attention; but as for there being more than this between this old couple, Lord Lucan assured me, and he was no prude, it was perfectly out of the question: and that anyone in the London Society of those days would have laughed at the possibility of anything else.

When the King went to Ireland a great opportunity was afforded for feminine display. This was of course grasped. When King William came to the throne he showed tact and good feeling. He requested that the very handsome presents, that had been made by the late King, of diamonds which were held to be those of the Crown, should not be returned to himself; but should be made into the splendid decoration of the Order of S' Patrick, still worn by the Lords Lieutenant of Ireland.

THE DUKE was frequently appealed to in matters of right and justice: it was felt not only that his judgment was most acute, but his calmness of decision perfect. On one occasion he received a letter in the following terms : I correct the spelling : "Mr Tomkins ventures to address the Duke of Wellingon. Mr Tomkins's mother is a washerwoman; Mr Tomkins regrets to say that, having washed for the Marquess of Douro for many years, his mother has been unable to obtain payment for the last three years. Mrs Tomkins is very poor ; and cannot afford to lose the money. She hopes the Duke will kindly pay it. Mrs Tomkins's address is . . . ."

After carefully reading and considering the letter, the Duke sent the following reply :

"Field Marshal The Duke of Wellington has received a letter from Mr Tomkins ; stating that the Marquess of Douro is in debt to his mother, Mrs Tomkins.

"The Duke of Wellington is not the Marquess of Douro.

"The Duke regrets to find that his eldest son has not paid his washerwoman's bill.

"Mrs Tomkins has no claim upon the Duke of Wellington.

"The Duke recommends her, failing another application, to place the matter in the hands of a respectable solicitor."

Some six weeks later the Duke had a dinner party at

Apsley House. One of the guests, with whom he was on intimate terms, introduced the subject of Autographs; and someone present asked the Duke if he was not tormented in this respect. The Duke replied "Oh, yes; constantly." The friend then said: "A few days ago I was examining a most interesting collection put together by a person who has laboured at it for many years. I saw your Grace's in the place of honour in his book." "Which was that?" said the Duke. "Well, the Collector's plan is to write to every person of eminence; and to accuse his eldest son of bilking his washerwoman. He pastes his own letter, and the reply, face to face."

I should like to have seen the Duke's face when he heard the first Prussian cannon at Waterloo: I should also like to have seen it on this occasion.

THE CONGRATULATORY address recited by Lord Maidstone afterwards Lord Winchilsea, at the Duke's Inauguration, as Chancellor of Oxford, was written by Dᵣ Bull, in my day Canon of Christ Church. It is quite worthless. The couplet

"Brought him to earth and tamed his tyrant wing
And closed our twenty years of suffering"

is very bad. The allusion to Rome, Carthage, Fabius, and Zama distract the hearers.

I cannot imagine anyone with good sense asking the question

> " Shall science in her pride a soldier spurn
> Say can she nothing from a soldier learn ? "

> " The light elastic loftiness of soul."

An elastic loftiness is worthy of the heavy old gentleman whom I recollect tottering into the Cathedral of Christ Church. Then follows :

> " To set at nought self-interest and ease
> These are their arts—and let us copy these !
> He ruled the state when dark and troublous round
> Gloomy and wild the dubious tempest frowned."

> " This will never do."

I must do Dr Bull justice : his figure on the south side of the Altar in our Christ Church Chapel, a Cathedral to the outside world, balanced by Dr Pusey on the north side, exemplified two types of Churchmen.

I admire him as a good logician ; as the following shows. Eating his luncheon, a Clergyman present

remarked that Canon Bull had not said grace : " I do
not say grace when the meal is cold."   " But, Sir, the
soup was hot."   " The heat of the soup was an accident, and not an essential, of the luncheon."

THE DUKE no doubt reckoned assassination
among the contingencies of his life. The attempt
by Cantillon in Paris on his return from Madame
Craufurd's soirée was a serious one ; and he received
frequent letters threatening a repetition of the crime.
It has always been considered that the bequeathment by Napoleon of a sum of money to Cantillon, the would-be murderer, was one of the worst
acts of his life. I saw the original will containing
this clause, when it was at Doctor's Commons;
the grammar bad ; the spelling incorrect ; and the
writing execrable. It must, however, be remembered
that this will was made at a time when Napoleon
was suffering under terrible gastric irritability; and
although he never, until a few hours before his
death, lost the complete command of his mind,
still it seems probable that this disposition was
made when he was hardly himself: at least one
must hope so. None knew better than Napoleon
that the Duke of Wellington had but little to do

with his punishment; that it was done by the Powers of Europe.

One incident has always struck me as most pictu- resque. When Napoleon's body lay, dressed in his uniform, on the bed on which he died, a yellow satin damask sofa cushion being placed under the head, the English garrison of St Helena marched past the body in single file. Each Commissioned Officer, as he passed, grasped the hand of the deceased soldier. The realities of History are infinitely more poetical than those of Fiction; and have much deeper senti- ment. This is one of them.

I may mention here that I have the cushion on which Napoleon's head was placed.

I have also his escritoire; and the chairs which he used at St Helena. The reader must not infer from this that I admire his character. Had he lived, I should have given them at the Tuileries to the poor lad, whose death was brought about by stupidity in the far off deserts of Africa.

LORD COMBERMERE was undoubtedly the best cavalry officer that the war had produced. The Duke was most anxious to have him at Waterloo; having long experience of his services in Spain;

and it was a cruel fate that deprived a man, who
had been so frequently engaged, and with such great
success, of the Command of the Cavalry on that
momentous day. The reason, I have heard on good
authority, was this. When the Duke of Wellington
was first sent to the Peninsula, Lord Anglesey, who
had rendered good service there, Commanding the
Cavalry, being senior to the Duke in the Army,
was obliged, of course, to go home. The Prince
Regent, feeling that Lord Anglesey was unfortunate,
promised him that whenever an opportunity occurred
he should command the British Cavalry. The Duke's
promotion to be a Field Marshal placed him above
Lord Anglesey in the Army List; and therefore at
Waterloo the same objection did not occur; and,
by the wish of the Prince Regent, Lord Anglesey
commanded the Cavalry.

SPLENDIDLY as the British troops fought; and
with a cheerfulness that excited the admiration of a
not very enthusiastic leader, the Duke must have
longed repeatedly during the Battle of the 18th for
his Army which broke up at Bordeaux. Of this
army he said repeatedly "They could go anywhere;
and do anything." Of these he had the nucleus of

twelve thousand admirable infantry ; and it is possible
that the confidence in these veterans of the Duke
felt by a younger race, may have combined with the
worship of their leader to achieve the glorious victory.

THE DUKE had won battle after battle. He had
marched from Cintra to Paris. He had routed all the
Generals opposed to him, one after another; he had
never lost a gun. Down to the youngest recruit, and
the boy Ensign who had joined the week before,
there was not one of his Army who did not believe in
him as being above humanity: there was not one
who ever doubted that the great man who was leading
them, was leading them to Conquest. This it was
that kept the men firm in their squares. They no
more believed that the French could beat them than
that they could fly over their heads.

I BELIEVE that no Army ever fought more bravely
than the French at Waterloo. I believe that their
courage on that day even transcended what Marengo,
Friedland, Jena, and Austerlitz showed : it is surprizing
that their commander, for whom they jeopardized
everything, seemed to think them unworthy of his

praise. They were simply "the broken tools" which
his Ambition "threw away."

IN ADDITION to its great political importance,
giving Europe a peace of forty years, Waterloo was a
fitting scene to terminate the Great Drama that
had been enacted for twenty-five years.

Beginning with the fall of the Bastille in 1789,
History presents nothing so interesting, nothing so
varied, as the struggle which ended on that Sunday
evening. The heroic death of the French Nobility,
who proved themselves worthy of their race on the
scaffold; the exceptional, and genuine piety of Louis
XVI.; the heroic character, and conduct of the
daughter of Maria Theresa; the fate of the little
Dauphin; combined to fill the Imagination of the
growing generation with hopes that Justice would at
last be done them. After long waiting, Retribution
came.

The Exiles, who had for the most part borne their
banishment with equanimity, returned to their an-
cestral homes; and the lawful King of France once
more entered the Tuileries.

Nothing could have shown the Duke of Wellington's tact, and well-bred feeling more than his

behaviour at this critical time. Never attempting
to thrust the Bourbons back upon the French people;
refusing even to advise them as to what they should
do : having freed their country of one who had
stripped every family in France of at least one of
its sons, he would play no active part in giving a
Sovereign to France. He knew human nature too
well : and though everything was owing to his
prowess, he always kept in the background. Giving
honest advice when asked, he never for a moment
assumed the part of a king-maker. He doubtless
recalled, in his dealing with worldlings, the cruel
words of Hobbes of Malmesbury "Obligation is Serfdom : inexpiable Obligation is eternal Serfdom."
Having studied with effect the character of the Bour-
bon family, he was too wise to let them feel, more
than could be helped, that they owed everything to
him. Content with the appreciation of the wise, and
sober portion of his countrymen, he felt that at last
Justice was being done him : and Retaliation for his
cruel wrongs did not fill his mind.

LORD CASTLEREAGH, moving a Vote of Thanks
to the Duke on the 23rd of June, 1815, said "One
feature of the Victory was that it had been gained

over the best troops of France; and that, too, at a moment when they displayed all their ardour; and when their conduct even surpassed all that they had before performed. This force did not amount to less than one hundred and thirty or one hundred and forty thousand men, the Flower of the French Army: which was a regular, and disciplined, army, even before the Bourbons quitted France; and for which, since the return of Bonaparte, everything had been done to make it effective. It was the force which had been selected, and combined, to act upon the Northern frontier."

The speech is feeble, and commonplace; and by no means worthy of the occasion. With all his talents Lord Castlereagh never was a good speaker. He says towards the end:

"Such was his" (the Duke's) "dauntless activity, that he was much more exposed than any private soldier, who could only bear the hazard of a single spot. The Duke was everywhere: at least wherever danger was."

IN A WORK published very shortly after the battle, in which allusion is made to Picton's reluctance to accept the command, it is said: "Since our army was sent to Flanders, the Government offered Sir Thomas Picton the command of a division; but, apprehending that the Duke of Wellington, as Commander in Chief, would leave the British force to some Officer in whom he could not repose the same confidence, he declined the offer; adding, however, that if the Duke should personally require his services, he would instantly repair to the army."

THE DUKE, like all men of sound intelligence, had a strong sense of humour; and I was delighted to find in a recent publication that the Duke occasionally read out, with great enthusiasm, and delight, Dickens's immortal description of the scene in Court of 'Bardell versus Pickwick.' I was so charmed with this acquisition to my knowledge of the Duke's character that I thought of it when going to sleep that night; and in that semi-dreaming condition, in which one is prone to be before absolute repose, I unconsciously mixed up Mrs Bardell, the Duke, Mr Winkle, Sergeant Snubbin, Mrs Cluppins, her umbrella, chops and tomato sauce, Sam Weller, Walmer Castle, warming pans; and even old Mr Weller in the gallery formed part of my half-dream.

Suddenly I had one of those extraordinary sensa-

tions, such as many of my readers must have felt
when they dream that they have fallen off a precipice,
and come to the ground. I awoke, as the French say,
"en sursaut"; with a shock never to be forgotten. It
flashed into my mind that there was a mysterious
connection between the phantoms of the Duke, and
Mᵣˢ Bardell; it was almost with pain that I recol-
lected all about it:

"And thrice ere the morning I dreamt it again."

At the very time of the Waterloo campaign, or
shortly afterwards, there can be no doubt that the
Duke was in the habit of addressing letters not unlike
those recently published, which we have read with
interest, to another young lady. So far, nothing could
be more innocent, nor more simple. No doubt he
wrote to her also equally graphic descriptions of the
leap-frog, kiss-in-the-ring, driving in goat-chaises, rug-
riding by ladies, etc., which was going on in the
Country House near Cambrai. All this showed a
playfulness, of which his nature was full. But unfortunately, this playfulness was expressed in writing; and
when the young, and gushing lady in question became
a decidedly elderly person, whom I knew well, and
who never married, the Duke received warnings of

a " Bardellian " character from the lady in question. I do not know whether any Dodson, or Fogg appeared on the scene. Imagination can picture nothing more awful, than the Great Duke, in a sweltering Court, listening to himself being denounced as a Monster of Iniquity by the Buzfuz of the period ; and held up to an envious, and delighted world as a fiend not to be surpassed : one to whom Don Juan was a St Anthony. Nothing so far as is popularly known, came of the affair. I have always had a suspicion that the half-sister of the lady, whom the Duke himself on one great occasion suspected of mischief, instigated these preliminary proceedings. The Christian name of the lady, which from exaggerated gentleness I do not mention, and who was of high rank, makes the Duke's conduct appear still more what ladies call "abominable."

THE FAMILY of Heath played a distinguished part in an earlier generation. One was the Head Master of Harrow, against whom the boys mutinied, in consequence of his being an Eton man, as I have mentioned ; the rebellion being headed by Lord Wellesley. Another was Head Master of Eton, previous to Dr Goodall. The third rose, I believe, to eminence in the law. A fourth, Baron Heath of the Kingdom of Italy, was Governor of the Bank of England. I knew the latter in his old age well. He was known as ' Barren Heath ': another was described as ' Black Heath '; and the Head Master of Eton as ' Ascot Heath.'

IT WAS said of the Duke that he knew so much that he thought he knew everything..

IT WAS also said that he spoke French as he fought; " bravement." No faults are to be found in the grammar of his written French.

I AVOIDED in my allusion to the Duke's ride from the Mint in 1832, to give particulars that have already been published. There is one however which has been omitted in the account published not long ago. It is related that the Duke watched with some anxiety the approach of a coal-waggon : what is not mentioned is, that when the Duke saw it approach, he said : " Hillo ! here's the Artillery coming up : we must look out."

THE DUKE, like all those whose intellects are exceptional, although he was surrounded to the last by those who gave him Appreciation, more valuable than Admiration, never can have found any one on a level with himself: and, until old age had defended him from Envy, must have felt that he was one of those

Who tread the friendless desert of success.

WITH AN honest wish to win the good opinion of sensible, and honourable men, the Duke was from first to last indifferent to the views of the multitude. He was by no means one of those

Who fancy Notoriety is Fame.

He accepted the great position to which his conduct had led; and wisely obtained so much enjoyment from it as he could. To pretend that he did not value his position would be absurd. He knew that he deserved what he had obtained; and appreciated his honours accordingly. The Duke felt that he could appeal to that loftiest of all tribunals, the Conscience of a Just, Wise, and Honourable man. The great pagan Poet Menander said,

To every man his Conscience is a God;

and the Duke could look inwards without fear.

THE NEWS of the death of Napoleon reached London on the 4^{tb} of July 1821. This was announced to George IV., with due solemnity, by the High Official on duty, in these words, befitting the occasion : " It is my duty to inform your Majesty that your greatest enemy is dead." " Is she by — " said the King.

THE DUKE never claimed for one moment credit to himself where he did not feel that it was thoroughly deserved. Someone saying to him : " How do you account, Duke, for your having so persistently beaten the French Marshals ? " The Duke simply replied " Well, the fact is their soldiers got them into scrapes : mine always got me out."

I HAVE compared the Duke with Frederick the Great of Prussia. He had all that Great Soldier's determination ; but where he had to act in a manner to give pain, I feel sure that the Duke did so with reluctance.

A story is told of the Great Frederick, from which a few words might have been recently taken with great effect : it fills me with astonishment that, of the millions who speak the great Teutonic language, no one thought of it.

In the midst of a severe action, Frederick rode past the spot where a young Officer, whom he knew well, and who had recently joined his Army, was writhing in the agonies of death. The King stopped; and heard some groans escaping the unfortunate boy. The King turned to him; and said, "Die silently, Frederick!"

Should not these words be placed on the tomb of one who obeyed the order of his great ancestor more than any man of whom we have read in History? Rapidly passing away as do the circumstances of life, his recent death can never be forgotten.

To have divided counsels, especially when the opposed counsellors are in earnest, is dreadful; and must have broken many a Monarch's heart: to lie on a sick bed, while Doctors dispute your real condition, and the character of the illness, is torture of the most exquisite kind to a sick man. What must it have been when both these sources of suffering were felt by the same person; and to know, in addition, that his Life, and Death were the objects of Political Intrigue!

All this was borne by the late German Emperor with a persistent, and calm Fortitude not to be surpassed in the records of Mankind. Let them write on his tombstone "STERBE STILL, FRITZ!"

OF THE DUKE it might be said that he was:

"In rebus adversis Magnus: in prosperis Bonus: utriusque fortunæ Dominus."

THE COURT of Napoleon the 1ˢᵗ, judging from their portraits, notwithstanding their splendid dresses, must have looked more or less like persons on the stage. Their coats, in the great pictures at Versailles, and elsewhere, never seem to fit them; they are too long in the sleeves. It must be a very difficult thing to improvise a number of courtiers, where there is no aristocratic tradition. The Duke, in whatever dress he was, whether in his various uniforms, the splendid robes of Chancellor of Oxford, or the Parliamentary, or Coronation robes of his rank, always looked worthy of the dress. You felt that however magnificent the apparel, the great man who wore it was grander still.

I SHOWED TO DISRAELI some lines on the Duke which Lord Stanhope gave me: he said "I must have written those forty years ago." They have since been published: and, for that reason only, I do not give them here.

I hope at some time to publish a volume containing my recollections of Disraeli, the intellectual successor of Lord Byron: and perhaps some unpublished facts anent the latter.

I SHOULD like to know what the Duke's grandparents were like; I believe that Genius, like gout, skips a generation. The Duke's father, Lord Mornington, was a Musician. With all his Genius, we cannot conceive the Duke composing a Cantata; nor writing a Sonnet.

A REAL LOVE letter of the Duke's would be priceless. I cannot imagine his writing one. Lord Byron, who found it very troublesome work, copied his out of " Les Liaisons Dangereuses "; and whenever a fresh innamorata appeared on the scene, she unconsciously received facsimiles of previous epistles.

ON ONE OCCASION George IV. persuaded the Duke to smoke: I believe that he never did this a second time.

THE DUKE owed nothing to his Mother.

" There is my ugly boy Arthur," Lady Mornington

said, on seeing him at the Dublin Theatre after a long absence.

The conventional notion that clever men have clever mothers is, I believe, a delusion : successful men have clever mothers. Most men pass the best years of their life in discovering what they are fit for. A mother who can place her son in the right groove ; tell him which talents to cultivate ; and show his Genius the road to success, may be sure that, should her son possess the qualities which she believes, her Glory will be great. This is very rarely the case.

I LATELY VISITED Londonderry House, formerly Holdernesse House, Park Lane, for evidence as to the Duke's Indian sword.

I have spoken of Frances Anne Lady Londonderry as the rival of Sarah Lady Jersey as a Queen of London Society. With more pretension, and a very imperious manner, which Lady Jersey had not, Lady Londonderry never had anything like Lady Jersey's power. "Frances Anne," at the tea-table covered with gold vessels, in the great gallery, was an awe-striking sight : but you felt that there was stage effect.

The 3rd Marquess, Frances Anne's husband, had rather too much of the old dandy, the Major Pendennis, for the brilliant soldier of the Peninsula. " Quel beau Sabreur !" had been then said of him.

His eldest son the 4th Marquess I knew well : he was the " Young Rapid " of H. B.'s " Equestrian Sketches."

A pathetic incident occurred in his childhood. His mother, Lord Londonderry's first wife, was writing a letter to his father, then abroad. She said to the boy of seven, " Write me something to send to Papa." The boy in a few minutes produced some lines headed " Epitaph on Poor Mamma": his mother was quite well. Lord Londonderry received the lines and the announcement of his Wife's death, at the same time.

The 5th Marquess was my brother officer : a most amiable, kind man ; a great sufferer.

My last visit was to look at the two fine pictures placed on the wall of the central hall of Londonderry House : they are of 'The Heroes of the Peninsula,' and 'The Heroes of Waterloo ': vigorously painted : the likenesses are good. They are by J. P. Knight.

The Duke in both wears the Indian sword.

On leaving the 1st Life Guards as a Captain I was made by the Officers an honorary member of their Mess ; a very exceptional distinction. Some years later the 1st Life Guards' Club was formed ; and in 1882,

I had the honour to be elected President. The Club
consists of Officers of the Regiment who are actually
serving, or have served; subject to exclusion if
thought proper. The locality of the Dinner is absolutely at the choice of the President for the year:
and is usually held at a City, or West End, Hotel.
Lord Londonderry, when he told me that his summer
duties with the Regiment of Yeomanry which he
commanded required his presence in Durham, most
kindly offered me Londonderry House for the evening. Nothing could be more splendid, nor more
picturesque than the large gallery lighted up for the
occasion: the summer evening's light coming in from
above. Seventy-three dined in the Gallery, in which
Pictures, and Statues, and all that is ornamental,
abound.

LORD CHARLES WELLESLEY, the Duke's second
son, the father of the present Duke, was sent from
Malta (I believe) with Dispatches of importance: he
reached London a fortnight later than he was expected.
The Duke, who supposed that he had loitered amid
the amusements of Paris, reprimanded him; and for
some days did not speak to his son.

Hearing accidentally that Lord Charles had been

delayed at Marseilles for the time lost, by Quarantine, he went up to him, after breakfast, and in the gentlest manner, pressing him to his breast, said, " Charles, you would like to hunt this winter, would you not ? " " I have no horses, Sir." " I have sent a thousand pounds to your Bankers, you can buy some."

I WROTE THE LINES on Orthez many years ago ; soon after my visit to ' La Belle Hôtesse.'

I received on the 13th of May last, from the Revd R. W., whom I did not know, a note addressed to him by Madame Bergereau, dated " Orthez ; le 6 Novembre, 1860." She says in it, " Wellington arrived at my Inn the 27th of February, 1814, (the day of the Battle of Orthez) at four o'clock in the afternoon, ' extenué de fatigue ; et mort de faim.' The Duke, with charming politeness, but *absolute insistance*, demanded food. I had nothing ; and told him so. He replied, ' On the contrary ; you have truffles ! smell for yourself !' I failed to smell any : the Duke, however, whose nose was sharper in every sense than mine, declared that he could not be mistaken : he triumphed : and a mass of truffles was found, of which I knew nothing. More than this ; pursuing his investigation, the Great Hero discovered, in a cupboard, a fine cooked turkey : it had been sent to a solicitor of Orthez, from Toulouse, as an annual present at Carnival time : the solicitor, refusing to pay the carriage, the Turkey had been lodged in my Hotel, as the bureau of the diligence." Madame Bergereau was a humourist. She adds : " I have said that the Duke's nose was sharper than mine : the weight of seventy years has not failed to sit upon my nose, as upon most things ; ' il s'affaisse, et s'elargit sous leur poids.' "

LORD WELLESLEY wrote these lines on his brother's Installation as Chancellor of the University of Oxford.

> "Conservata tuis Asia, atque Europa, Triumphis
>   Invictum Bello te coluere Ducem :
> Nunc umbrata geris Civili tempora Quercu ;
>   Ut desit Famæ Gloria nulla tuæ."

> Asia hath seen thy conquering Sword ;
> And Europe's Laurels crown her Lord :
> Now, round thy brows the Oak we twine ;
> That every Glory may be thine.

W. F.

I HAD THE GLAD FORTUNE to hear, as a Member of Parliament, the following speech, delivered on the Vote for the Duke's Funeral.

The House of Commons was crowded to the ceiling: the seats, and galleries, of the Members were full: and almost every distinguished man in England was present.

"THE QUEEN'S MESSAGE CONSIDERED."

"THE CHANCELLOR OF THE EXCHEQUER (MR. DISRAELI) rose and said Mr. Speaker: Sir, The House of Commons is called upon to-night to perform a sorrowful, but a noble duty. It has to recognize, in the face of the Country and of the Civilized World, the loss of the most distinguished of our Citizens; and it has to offer to the ashes of the great departed the solemn anguish of a Bereaved Nation.

"Sir, the Princely Personage who has left us was born in an age more fruitful of great events than any other period of recorded time. Of its vast incidents the most conspicuous were his own deeds: deeds achieved with the smallest means; and against the greatest obstacles.

"He was, therefore, not only a Great Man, but the Greatest Man of a Great Age.

"Amid the chaos, and conflagration which attended

the close of the last century there arose one of those beings who seem born to master Mankind. It is not too much to say that Napoleon combined the imperial ardour of Alexander with the strategy of Hannibal.

"The Kings of the earth fell before his fiery and subtle Genius: and at the head of all the Powers of Europe, he denounced destruction against the only land that dared to disobey him, and be free.

"The Providential Superintendence of the World seems scarcely ever more manifest than when we recollect the dispensations of our day: that the same year which gave to France the Emperor Napoleon, produced also for us the Duke of Wellington; that in the same year they should have embraced the same profession; and that, natives of distant islands, they should both have repaired for their military education to that illustrious land which each in his turn was destined to subjugate. During that long struggle for our Freedom, our Glory, I might say for our Existence, Wellesley fought, and won, fifteen pitched battles; all of them of the highest class; concluding with one of those crowning Victories that give a colour, and a form to History. During that period, that can be said of him which can be said of no other Captain; *that he captured three thousand cannon from the enemy; and never lost a single gun.*

" The greatness of his exploits was, perhaps, even surpassed by the difficulties which he had to encounter. He had to encounter a feeble Government ; a factious Opposition; a distrustful people; scandalous allies; and the most powerful enemy in the world.

" He won Victories with starving troops ; and he carried on Sieges without Munitions.

" As if to complete the fatality which attended him throughout life in this respect, when he had at last succeeded in creating an Army worthy of the Roman Legions, and worthy of himself, this Invincible Host was broken up on the eve of the greatest conjuncture of his life : he had to enter the Field of Waterloo with raw levies, and discomfited Allies.

" But the star of Wellington never paled.

" He has been called fortunate ; but Fortune is a Divinity which has ever favoured those who are, at the same time, Sagacious and Intrepid; Inventive and Patient. It was his own Character that created his Career; alike achieved his exploits; and guarded him from every vicissitude : for it was his sublime Self-controul alone that regulated his lofty Fate.

"Sir, it has been of late years somewhat the fashion to disparage the Military Character. Forty years of Peace have, perhaps, made us somewhat less aware how considerable, and how complex, are the qualities which go to the formation of a Great General.

"It is not enough that he must be an Engineer, a Geographer, learned in Human Nature, and adroit in managing men: he must also be able to fulfil the highest duty of a Minister of State; and then to descend to the humblest office of a Commissary, and clerk: and he has to display all this knowledge, and to exercise all these duties, at the same time; and under extraordinary circumstances. At every moment he has to think of the eve, and of the morrow; of his flank, and of his rear. He has to carry with him Ammunition, Provisions, and Hospitals. He has to calculate at the same time the state of the weather, and the moral qualities of man: and all these elements, that are perpetually changing, he has to combine; sometimes under overwhelming heat; and sometimes under overpowering cold: sometimes even amid famine; and often amid the roar of Artillery. Behind all these circumstances, too, there is ever present the image of his country; and the dreadful alternative, whether that country is to welcome him with the Laurel, or the Cypress. Yet this image he must dismiss from his mind ; for the General must think ; and not only think ; he must think with the rapidity of lightning ; for on a moment more or less depends the fate of a most beautiful combination : and on a moment more or less depends the question of Glory, or of Shame. Unquestionably, Sir, all this might be done in an ordinary manner, and by an ordinary man ; as, every day of our lives, we see ordinary men who may be successful Ministers of State, successful Authors, successful Speakers : But to do all this with Genius is Sublime. Doubtless, to be able to think with Vigour, with Clearness, and with Depth, in the recess of The Cabinet, is a fine intellectual demonstration : but to think with equal Vigour, Clearness, and Depth, amidst bullets, appears the loftiest exercise and the most complete triumph of the human faculties.

"Sir, when we take into consideration the prolonged, and illustrious life of the Duke of Wellington, we are surprized how small a section of that life is occupied by that military career which fills so large a space in history. Only eight years elapsed from Vimiera to Waterloo ; and from the date of his first commission to the last cannon-shot which he heard on the Field of Battle, scarce twenty years can be counted.

R

" After all his triumphs he was destined for another career; and the greatest, and most successful of warriors, if not in the prime, at least in the perfection of Manhood, commenced a civil career scarcely less successful, scarcely less splendid, than that military one which will live for ever in the memory of men.

" He was thrice the Ambassador of his Sovereign at those great historic Congresses that settled the affairs of Europe : twice was he Secretary of State : twice he was Commander-in-Chief of the Forces : once he was Prime Minister of England : and to the last hour of his life he may be said to have laboured for his country.

" It was only a few months before we lost him that he favoured with his counsel, and assistance the present advisers of the Crown respecting that war in the East, of which no one could be so competent to judge : He drew up his views on that subject in a State Paper characterized by all his Sagacity, and Experience : and, indeed, when he died, he died still the active chieftain of that famous Army, to which he has left the Tradition of his Glory.

" Sir, there is one passage in the life of the Duke of Wellington, which in this place, and on this occasion, I ought not to let pass unnoticed. It is our pride that he was one of ourselves : it is our glory that Sir

Arthur Wellesley once sat on these benches. If we view his career in the House of Commons by the tests of success which are applied to common men, his career, although brief, was still distinguished.

"He entered the Royal Councils ; and filled high offices of State. But the success of Sir Arthur Wellesley in the House of Commons must not be tested by the facts that he was a Privy Councillor; or a Secretary of a Lord Lieutenant. He achieved here a great success which the greatest Ministers, and the most brilliant Orators may never hope to accomplish. That was a great Parliamentary triumph, when he rose in his place to receive the thanks of Mr. Speaker for a brilliant victory : and, later still, when at that bar to receive, Sir, from one of your predecessors in memorable words, the thanks of a grateful Senate for accumulated triumphs.

"Sir, there is one source of consolation which I think the people of England possess at this moment under the severe bereavement over which they mourn : It is their intimate acquaintance with the character, and even the person, of this great man. There never was a man of such mark who lived so long, and so much, in the public eye.

"I will be bound there is not a Gentleman in this

House who has not seen him : many there are who have conversed with him : some there are who have touched his hand. His Image, his Countenance, his Manner, his Voice are impressed on every memory and sound almost in every ear.

"In the golden saloon, and in the busy market-place, to the last he might be found.

"The rising generation among whom he lived will often recall his words of kindness : and the people followed him in the street with that lingering gaze of reverent admiration, which seemed never to tire. Who, indeed, can ever forget that venerable, and classic head, ripe with Time ; and radiant as it were with Glory?

"'Stilichonis apex et cognita fulsit
Canities.'

"To complete all, that we might have a perfect idea of his inward, and spiritual nature ; that we might understand how this Sovereign Master of Duty fulfilled the manifold offices of his life with unrivalled Activity, he himself gave us a collection of Military, and Administrative Literature, which no Age, and no Country can rival. And, fortunate in all things, Wellington found in his lifetime an Historian, whose immortal page now ranks with the classics of that land which Wellesley saved.

" Sir, the Duke of Wellington has left to his Country a great Legacy; greater even than his Fame : he has left to them the contemplation of his Character.

" I will not say of England that he has revived here the Sense of Duty : that, I trust, was never lost. But that he has inspired Public Life with a purer and more masculine tone, I cannot doubt : that he has rebuked by his career restless Vanity ; and regulated the morbid susceptibility of irregular Egotism, is, I think, no exaggerated praise.

" I do not believe that among all orders of Englishmen, from the highest to the lowest, from those who are called on to incur the most serious responsibilities of Office, to those who exercise the humblest duties of Society, I do not believe there is one among us who may not experience moments of doubt and depression ; when the image of Wellington will occur to his Memory, and he finds in his example Support, and Solace.

" Although the Duke of Wellington lived so much in the minds, and hearts of the people of England ; although at the end of his long career he occupied such a prominent position, and filled such august offices; no one seemed to be conscious of what a space he occupied in the thoughts and feelings of his countrymen, until he died.

" The influence of true Greatness was never, perhaps, more completely asserted than in his decease.

" In an Age in which the belief in intellectual equality flatters so much our self-complacency, every one suddenly acknowledges that the world has lost its foremost man.   In an age of Utility, the most busy, and the most common-sense people in the world find no vent for their woe ; and no representative for their sorrow ; but the solemnity of a pageant ; and we, who are assembled here for purposes so different ; to investigate the sources of the Wealth of Nations ; to busy ourselves in Statistical Research ; to encounter each other in fiscal controversy ; we offer to the World the most sublime, and touching spectacle that human circumstances can well produce ; the Spectacle of a Senate mourning a Hero."

WATERLOO.

LEAVING BRUSSELS on a fine afternoon in August, 1888, I reached the little station near Braine l'Alleud in half an hour ; and thence drove to the Hôtel du Musée, close to the Prince of Orange's mound. This horrible disfigurement of the Plain of Waterloo has materially altered the defensive position taken by the Duke of Wellington. Well might he say, when visiting the spot some years after the battle, "They have spoiled my Battle-field."

A high ridge extended along the greater part of the British front : the removal of this to form the Mound has given quite a different character to this part of the scene. The Hôtel du Musée is situated near the right centre of the British line.

I ordered a carriage to be ready at four o'clock to take me to Quatre-Bras : In the meantime I walked in an easterly direction over the battle-field. The old pavé from Brussels passes through the Villages of

Waterloo, and Mont S⁺ Jean, in the rear of the British centre. In former days the Museum, now at the Hotel, which was principally formed by Sergeant-Major Cotton of the 7ᵗʰ Hussars, who acted as orderly to Sir Hussey Vivian, commanding a Brigade of Light Cavalry, on the 18ᵗʰ June, was in his house, in Mont S⁺ Jean.

A circumstance, very interesting to myself, occurred on my first visit to Waterloo. This was before I had left Eton; and just previous to my going to Oxford. Sergeant-Major Cotton, who was an excellent, and intelligent guide, and who had acquired a vast amount of information from having traversed the field with the distinguished Officers who had taken part in the battle, showed us over Hougomont; and pointed out in the kitchen-garden, which still adjoins the orchard, the grave-stone where my cousin, Captain Thomas Craufurd of the 3ʳᵈ Guards, was killed. He was most unfortunate; for I believe he was almost, if not quite, the only Officer slain inside the enclosure. The brick wall, which is still pierced with loop-holes protected the troops, in a great measure. The south line of wall was defended by the Coldstream Guards. Craufurd occupied the little kitchen garden, on their right flank, with a detachment of the 3ʳᵈ Guards.

Cotton, who did not know who I was at the time, told me that he had seen many sad sights; but that the saddest he had ever seen was that of Sir James Craufurd weeping over his son's grave. Thence I walked across the fields to Cotton's house; in which there was a large collection of arms, uniforms, etc., etc., found after the battle; in addition to some things that had been presented to, or been purchased by him. Looking about I saw hanging on the wall, high up, a Sword; to which was attached a card somewhat soiled by time. I read on it "Sword worn by Lieut.-Colonel Sir James Fraser B¹, 7ᵗʰ Hussars, at Waterloo." I asked to be allowed to examine it; and I then said to Cotton "I should like to purchase that sword; but before I make you an offer, it is only fair to tell you who I am, as it will add to the value: Sir William Fraser." He seemed startled; and said "Sir James's son?" "Yes." I said to him "What will you take?" He replied "Sir William, I am fairly well off, and I don't want to part with the sword." I said "I will give you twenty-five pounds." He declined. I then said "Thirty; forty; fifty pounds?" He replied "No; I must give you the same answer; I do not wish to part with the sword." I then said "If you should ever part with the sword, I hope you will give me the first opportunity of buying it; and will not let it go into other hands." He said "You may rely on it, that, should I ever decide to sell it, I will let you know." About a year afterwards I wrote from Oxford. I reminded him that both he and I were mortal; and that the loss of such a sword to my family would be irreparable. I desired him to name his price: he replied that he would accept my first offer, *i.e.* twenty-five pounds. I obtained the sword. Cotton was then in full, vigorous health; he died soon afterwards. I have the sword now.

So much for the past.

AT FOUR O'CLOCK I started for Quatre-Bras. Passing close to the farm of 'La Haye Sainte,' of which more hereafter; the road is through the hamlet of 'Vieux Genappes': I stopped at a house called "La Maison du Caillou." I was reluctant to ask permission of the owner to see the house. However, he most courteously admitted me at once. M. Emile Coulon, the owner, an Architect of eminence, was so very polite as to show me everything that was of interest. He pointed out to me the bed-room

in which Napoleon slept on the night of the 17th
of June; the table upon which he breakfasted with
Marshals Soult, and Ney; and the two tables upon
which he spread his maps. These three are exceptionally beautiful; the proprietor has had a drawing
of them registered in the most formal manner. I
begged him, in addition to this, to have a small plate
attached to each; and I sincerely hope that he has
done, or will do, this. M. Coulon took me into the
kitchen garden, from the northern angle of which
Napoleon first saw the battle-field in the distance.
He also pointed out to me what was most interesting,
the line of country taken by Napoleon, and his personal Staff, when riding away from the field, on the
evening of the 18th. A large meadow intervenes
between the road, which was then blocked with wag-
gons etc., and the line which Napoleon took across
country. A very remarkable conversation took place
during this ride.

Continuing, I reach Genappes, a flourishing, busy
town, with clean streets, and a look of vitality about
it very different from the old towns of Belgium.
Crossing the narrow bridge, which spans the little
river, hardly more than a canal, I was astonished,
and am still, as to how four armies could have

crossed it in the time occupied by them. On the
17th of June the British, and French armies crossed
it : on the 18th the French Army, followed by the
Prussian Army, recrossed the bridge. Another surprizing fact is that within half a mile there is
another bridge across the river, which was not used
by any one man of the three armies. When Lacoste,
Napoleon's guide, was asked why he did not lead the
Emperor over this bridge, the latter having requested
him to show him the shortest way to Charleroi, he
simply replied : " I knew nothing about the bridge."
It seems incredible that in a country, destined, as
was well known before, to be, and as it had been, the
" Cock-pit of Europe," the fact that there was a
second available bridge was unknown to both Com-
manders. Continuing from Genappes, Quatre-Bras
was reached. The little hamlet at first appeared to
be deserted. I could find no one. At last I came
upon the inhabitants, collected apparently in a sort of
club at the common inn, situated at the angle of four
roads. They repudiated all knowledge of the battle ;
in fact declared that there had been no battle there.
They pointed over their shoulders, meaning that there
had been fighting at Waterloo ; of which I told them
that I had heard something ; but they persisted in

the statement that there had been no engagement at Quatre-Bras : Such is Fame !

I walked slowly down the Nivelles Road, and was shortly overtaken by a Belgian farmer ; who showed what I have frequently noticed in the provincial districts of Belgium, great personal courtesy. I have never been in any country where passers-by treat strangers with more respect. He kindly offered to show me what I wished to see : pointing out the spot where the Duke of Brunswick fell. I may here say that when I mentioned in a letter, which will follow, that the Duke of Brunswick "fell as his father fell," I did not say die, as his father died ; but was wounded almost precisely in the same part of his body, dying in half an hour; his father being carried, after the battle of Jena, in a litter a considerable distance, to Ottensen, a suburb of Altona, near Hamburg.

THE BATTLE-FIELD of Quatre-Bras is plain enough. The Bois de Bossu, the scene of such severe fighting, and carnage, exists no more : there is not a trace of it. It was in this wood that revolting barbarity was perpetrated. The Highlanders had been driven out for a few minutes only : on recapturing the wood they found that their dead, and wounded comrades had been mutilated in the most horrible manner. The Highland dress was the object of the real, or affected ridicule of the French : a ridicule which they were induced to repent two days afterwards.

THE BARN with its yard, in which the Duke was nearly captured, is as it was ; in fact I should say that very little change has taken place in the few buildings adjacent to the field. I am very glad to take this opportunity of repeating the thanks, which I gave M. Brasseur, Fermier, de Quatre-Bras, for his kindness, and courtesy, in showing me over the field. Had it not been late, and the evening very cold, I should have been glad to visit his farm, to which he was so kind as to invite me.

RETURNING through Genappes, I examined carefully the upper part of the town ; where an encounter had taken place on the 17th of June. It is surprizing that Napoleon did not follow up the British on their retirement to Waterloo. The Duke of Wellington said "Napoleon is not there; or he would not have allowed me to get through the town so easily." My own impression is that the defeat of the French at

Quatre-Bras was more severe than is generally thought. I also believe that the reason why Napoleon did not follow up the battle of Ligny, which he certainly won, was that the Prussians did not sustain so severe a defeat as is generally believed.

In the rear of the army that had passed through Genappes on the 17th of June was the 7th Regiment of Hussars, associated, I am proud to say, with my family; my father having served in it for twenty-five years, and commanded the Regiment; my brother having been Major; and in which my nephew now serves as Lieutenant. With imprudence Lord Anglesey, who was Colonel-in-Chief of the Regiment, and who had long served in it, hurled them against a dense mass of Lancers, very heavy troops, who had just emerged from Genappes.

The 7th Hussars could naturally produce no impression upon them; with their short, curved swords, and the comparatively light horses, they fell away as water from a wall. Not only were they checked, but a squadron captured; General Robbins telling me, that the fact of his escape was due to his riding a powerful hunter which he had bought in Dorsetshire the year previous: by this means he was enabled to clamber up a high bank. Two officers were

taken.   Lord Anglesey then ordered the 1st Life
Guards to stop the Lancers.   They attacked in column,
the rear rank of the rear troop charging first.   They
made very short work of the French Cavalry, and so
effectually stopped their approaches that the Army was
unmolested; and able to take up its position on the
Plain of Waterloo.   The following incident happened
on the evening of the 17th.   The two officers, who had
been taken in the affair just mentioned, were brought
before Napoleon.   Standing near his chair was Count
Flahault, his A.D.C., who had been in London during
the First Restoration : and, being a handsome young
Frenchman, of good birth, and manners, had been
made a great deal of in London society.   Wishing, I
assume, to show to the Emperor, his master, that he
had been by no means inoculated with a love for the
British race, he said something, what I do not know,
that was considered offensive by the British officers.
Although Count Flahault subsequently married his
relation, Miss Elphinstone, the daughter of Admiral
Lord Keith, in her own right Baroness Keith and
Nairne, Mr Elphinstone and Count Flahault never
spoke to one another to the end of their lives.

I returned to the Hôtel du Musée an hour after
dark.   The next morning I walked over to Hougo-

mont. I may point out here a long-standing evil;
which I think the Belgian Government ought to
remove. They could do so without difficulty. I refer
to the beggars, who, under the guise of selling sticks,
pester everyone who goes in and out of the Hotel.
It is disgraceful that such a state of things should be
permitted; and I feel sure that their persistency, with
the proximity of sticks, must not unfrequently lead to
breaches of the peace.

I found the Château of Hougomont renovated; but
not seriously altered.

It is a very strong position : its occupation by the
Division which held the buildings, and their rear, is
easily understood.

The dense wood, which existed at the time of the
Battle to the south of the building and enclosures, is
now entirely gone.

When I first visited Waterloo there were some
remains of this wood; some stumps of trees riddled
with shot; but even these have now disappeared.

About fifteen yards distant from the south front of
the enclosure are a hedge and ditch. The former
has grown up again since Waterloo ; and forms an
excellent screen. The British Guards were able to
fire through the loop-holes of the south wall, and

through this screen of hedge into the French column headed by King Joseph Bonaparte; the French being entirely unable to see their adversaries; indeed there can be little doubt that they persisted in firing at the brick wall from whence our fire issued, under the impression that it was a line of British Infantry. The loop-holes are still in the wall: and, although the top of the wall has been repaired, it is materially in the same condition in which it was on the day of the battle.

A considerable part of the Château, as is well known, was burned by the French shells. The Chapel still remains, in which, I am sorry to say, half a dozen "'arrys" were howling. On entering the gate, I walked at once into the orchard; and climbing over the low wall, which separates the little kitchen garden from the orchard, I found that the whole space of the kitchen garden which, when I formerly saw it, was in an utterly neglected condition, was covered with vegetables. The stone which I saw there on my two previous visits, placed on Captain Thomas Craufurd's grave, was gone. I remember perfectly that there was an inscription on it, stating his name, and that he had fallen on that spot. I could see no trace of the stone: it has been removed, I am quite certain without

the knowledge of the proprietor, in order to make
room for a few more beans.

As regards the heavy doors, formerly under a brick
arch which has fallen down, in the rear of the buildings
of Hougomont, which were closed by Sir James Macdonnell, and Sergeant Graham, it is well known that
the Duke handed the legacy bequeathed to the bravest
man in the British Army to Sir James Macdonnell,
as having shown the most useful courage that the
Duke could think of. Sir James Macdonnell insisted
upon sharing it with Sergeant Graham; and I am glad
to have been able to ascertain his name. He was a
sergeant of the Coldstream Regiment of Guards. His
name has lately been published as Fraser : but, I believe, in error.

The younger brother of Captain Thomas Craufurd
of Kilbirnie, whom I have mentioned as having
been killed at Hougomont, was extra A.D.C. to
Sir William Ponsonby unfortunately killed while
endeavouring to restrain the charge of the well-
known Union Brigade.

The British Cavalry on that day performed deeds
of valour, and prowess that will for ever live in history ;
but their horses were fresh ; and the men were eager
for the fray. Entirely unexhausted by a previous cam-

paign, they had but one idea, to ride to the front ; and
annihilate the French army. This unhappily in several
instances led to the almost entire destruction of these
fine Regiments.

It was the Duke's wish to keep his Cavalry well in
reserve. He knew that the Infantry would, as they
did, withstand the shock of the French attacks : and
certain as he was that sooner or later an opportunity
would be given him to advance, it was his hope that a
strong, fresh body of cavalry would quicken the departure of the French.

Passing from Hougomont, across the fields in a
state of wonderful fertility, I examined the outside
of the farm of ' La Haye Sainte.'

The inevitable "amari aliquid" seems to have
arisen in the Duke's mind as regards this fortress.
Numerous as are the descriptions of this block of
buildings ; and simple as was the matter, errors have
been made.

The cause of its capture by the French in the afternoon has been attributed to the absence of an opening in the wall on the north side of the enclosure.
This wall is not above one hundred and fifty yards from
the front of the British line ; and, looking at a plan
or map, it seems incredible that it could not be

reached. Some accounts state that there is a small door in the rear of the building; others relating that there is not. The fact is this; in addition to the principal entrance, which opens on to the road towards Genappes, there is a small door towards the rear of the building; but it is at the side of the rear, or rather at the rear of the east side: and opens, like the large one, on to the road. This road was swept by the French guns: and it was absolutely impossible to reach it from the British line. Had there been an opening in the wall, immediately at the rear, the building itself would have covered the approach of a small and determined body of men; but enfiladed as both doors were, no one could get near them.

At the same time it surprizes me that, with the powder contained in the cartridges, the fine Hanoverian corps who defended it so gallantly for many hours, and perished almost to a man, could not blow a hole in the wall at the rear of their little fortress. I heard many years ago that it was not the case that their final surrender was caused by this defect: but that the cartridges, which were carried to them through a desperate fire, were found not to fit their rifles. I suspect that this was really the case: being of a different service, this might well have occurred. The Duke, when asked the question, at first said that the Prince of Orange commanded the Division ; and ought to have attended to it : he immediately corrected himself, however, and said "No ; it was my fault : but one cannot think of everything." Could generosity go further ? A man with his vast responsibility actually blamed himself for a detail : thereby showing, as he did at every opportunity, the noble unselfishness of his nature.

As regards many stories told of things that he did on that day, they bear the semblance of truth. The Duke said that he could not remember whether he wore a cloak on the 18th. He said he did on the 17th, for it rained. In the afternoon of the 18th, I have this on good authority, he took off his cloak, and Sir William de Lancy, who was his Q.-M. General, and his most intimate friend, in order not to put the Duke to inconvenience, dismounted ; and was fastening the Duke's cloak to the front of his own saddle, when he was struck down : he most unfortunately gave orders to those who were carrying him from the field, to leave him there ; and to go back, and fight. He was found alive the next morning ; and his life might possibly have been saved under other circumstances. He died some days later in Brussels.

It is related of the Duke that on one occasion, when the French were advancing, he entered a Square; chatted quietly with the Commanding Officer, and said "Oh, it will be all right: if the Prussians come up in time we shall have a long peace."

The fine, stiff-necked Colonel, mounted in the centre of Mrs Butler's spirited picture of "A Square at Quatre Bras," is, I should say, taken from a portrait, which I have, of Cameron of Lochiel; not of course of his Regiment. His neatly arranged wig, and whiskers, are utterly different from the conventional idea of a wild Highlander.

IT WOULD FAR exceed the limits of this volume to go into the various questions of the Duke's strategy, and tactics. A great deal of nonsense has been talked, and written on the subject. Napoleon is reported to have said at St Helena that the Duke was at fault in taking up a position in front of a forest, which at that time extended from Waterloo to Brussels. Now it is nearly all gone. Napoleon ought to have defined what he meant by the term "forest." To take up a position in front of a forest, that has the character of a jungle, full of impassable underwood, would certainly be very imprudent. The Forest of Soignies was nothing of the sort. It was a wood of pine trees; than which there is nothing more easy for troops to traverse or defend; no underwood: and not only no obstacle to their retreat, but it would have proved the most admirable means for their defence.

In addition to this, three good roads led through this wood. The Duke would not allow a wheel-barrow to block these means of retreat. He could have used them without any difficulty.

The Duke intended to move, not towards Brussels, but towards the West. His first object was to keep up his communication with the sea: and with the great fortress of Antwerp.

It was for this reason that he placed a 'corps d'armée' under Lord Hill on the right flank of his own army; in order that, had it been necessary to retire from his position, he could have done so, without difficulty, in that direction. Lord Hill's force would have afforded protection; and had the French endeavoured to press upon the Duke, this part of the whole force, which was absolutely unfatigued, combined with the Prussians, who he knew perfectly well must come up sooner or later, would have entirely prevented Napoleon penetrating to Brussels.

People who are in the habit of speaking without

thinking, or who are incapable of thought, have said that if the Prussians had not come up the British Army must have been annihilated. More perfect nonsense never was uttered.

Had the Duke not known that the Prussian Army was where it was, he would never have fought the battle. Every movement that he made was in accord with the fact that the Prussians were near him. Napoleon said "La guerre est une affaire de jambes autant que de courage": had it not been for the overwhelming deluge of rain which fell on the previous day and night, the whole Prussian force would have been on the flank of the French at four o'clock in the afternoon, or soon after.

To anyone who will take the trouble to spend half an hour in examining the map; to say nothing of the easy method of walking over the field itself; it is perfectly clear that the Duke had arranged matters with the perfection of wisdom. No human being could tell the secret, which was in Napoleon's breast alone, as to how he would advance from his own country into Belgium. The probabilities were that he would come by Mons, and Hal. That seemed to give him the best opportunity of reaching Brussels, which was his *political* object. Wishing, above all, to convince

·the French people that he was still invincible, he desired to obtain possession of the Belgian Capital.

This was his first object ; thinking thereby that the people of France would again allow levies to be raised ; and that he might be able to carry on a desperate, and possibly successful War. This was the cause of his hurrying towards the Belgian frontier. The Duke of Wellington has said that he ought to have waited ; and that " Napoleon never had patience enough to fight a defensive war." It does however, notwithstanding this dictum, seem probable that his first object was political. His newly regained throne was, as he well knew, tottering under him. He had the French *Army* with him ; not the French *People.* He was as a gambler playing his last stake ; and nothing but a brilliant, and immediate success would have enabled him to remain Emperor of France.

Impossible as it clearly was for the Duke to know by which route Napoleon intended to advance, he posted his troops on the various roads in such con-tiguity that each corps d'armée could help the others. So soon as he ascertained the line of Napoleon's ad-vance he took steps to check him ; and succeeded.

IT HAS been said, with a view to disparage the

Duke, that he was not prepared for Napoleon's attack. A very few minutes' consideration will put an end to this idea. There were three principal roads leading from the French frontier to Brussels. That on the east by Namur; that in the centre by Charleroi; that on the west by Mons. No human being but Napoleon knew by which of these roads Brussels would be attacked. The Duke took every possible precaution to guard these three roads. If the reader will place the three central fingers of his, or her, right hand on this page, the matter can very easily be explained. Let the reader assume that the centre of the knuckles represents Brussels; the forefinger to represent the road from Namur; the central finger from Charleroi; the third finger from Mons.

The Duke posted troops on each of these roads, say at the first joint from the point of each finger.

So soon as it was known that Napoleon was advancing from Charleroi, that is, by the central finger, the British and Prussian armies were, so far as possible, brought together, at the first joint of that finger. Quatre-Bras, and Ligny were there fought on the 16th of June. In consequence of the Prussian army being driven back, it became necessary for the British army, in order to effect a junction with them, to retire to the plain of Waterloo, that is, the second joint of the central finger. There the Battle was fought on the 18th.

AMONG OTHER absurd questions this has been asked. "What would have happened if the Prussians had not come up?" The reply to this is very simple. The Battle would not have been fought. The Duke arranged everything with the Commander in Chief of the Prussian Army, Marshal Blucher; he had surveyed the country the year before; and had made memoranda showing where the Battle must be fought. It was absolutely certain that the Prussian army must, sooner or later, join his own. The Duke had asked Marshal Blucher for one Division of 25,000 men. Blucher promised this; and kept his word. Blucher also promised, without the Duke suggesting it, that the whole of his army should join the Duke's, and attack the French right flank so early as possible. Bulow's Division arrived between three and four, according to promise; and also according to promise, Marshal Blucher joined with his main army so soon as the desperate condition of the roads from rain permitted.

IT HAS BEEN SAID that the detachment of a corps

d'armée to the west, which took no part in the battle, was faulty; that this corps d'armée was useless. It is surprizing how much ignorance, or malignity can be shown. I consider that the corps d'armée detached to the west answered three distinct purposes. The First, that it blocked the road from Mons, by which it might reasonably be supposed Napoleon would attempt to advance upon Brussels. In fact, on the night of the 17th Napoleon detached 2,000 cavalry on this very road. They found their path stopped; and returned to the main army. The Second object of the position of the corps d'armée was to intercept the French : had they been driven back by the Prussians under circumstances which would have prevented the British Army from attacking them at the same moment. Had the French right front, which fought ' en potence,' that is to say, thrown back; and which became their front towards the Prussians, been compelled to retreat, this western corps d'armée would have prevented their escape; and they would have found themselves placed between two fires; a hopeless position. The Third great object of the detachment of the corps d'armée to the west, was to enable the Duke to pass in that direction, had he been unable to defeat the French ; this detached corps d'armée protecting his left flank. The Duke's best troops were landing daily on the west coast. These appear to me to be the reasons, simply expressed, for the Duke acting as he did.

IN THE DUKE'S official account of the battle, dated "Waterloo, June 19, 1815," the last paragraph but one is as follows : "The operation of General Bulow upon the enemy's flank was a most decisive one : and even if I had not found myself in a situation to make the attack which produced the final result, it would have forced the Enemy to retire if his attacks should have failed; *and would have prevented him from taking advantage of them if he should unfortunately have succeeded."* These last words should be learned by heart. They explain the situation with absolute clearness.

ORDERS WERE SENT to clear the bridge at Genappes at five o'clock in the afternoon of Waterloo. I have lately heard that a very distinguished French soldier, with good means of knowing the facts, has stated that Napoleon knew that he was defeated at three o'clock; in fact the failure of his first attack of Horse, Foot, and Artillery must have shown him the extreme difficulty of penetrating the British position.

WHEN NAPOLEON was told that the advancing Prussians were Grouchy coming up at last, he looked through his opera-glass; and said " No, no : black is black ; and blue is blue ; those are Prussians."

THE GREATEST MEN have probably owed their ultimate success to promotion in early life. Julius Cæsar was the nephew of Marius : Napoleon married a friend of Barras: the Duke of Wellington was Lord Wellesley's brother.

WHAT MUST HAVE BEEN the Duke's feelings of honest triumph when Lord Grey who, after the failure at Burgos, had denounced him in unmeasured terms, declared in a speech in the Duke's presence, in the House of Lords, that in his, Lord Grey's, opinion the Duke's character transcended that of every ancient, and modern hero.

THE CARDINAL DE RETZ declared that the great Marquess of Montrose was the only man who equalled the Pagan Heroes : having the ideal virtues

of Classic Times. What would he have said of
Wellington ?

AMONG THE INCIDENTS OF WATERLOO,
it is startling to find that Bulow's Division, whose
advent first alarmed Napoleon, might have completely
failed but for the judgment of a single Belgian peasant.
On leaving the woods of Frischermont, to the right
of the French army, two roads diverge. The man
who guided the Column hesitated: and for a few
minutes considered which path he should take. He
chose the left one; saying " Now we shall take them
all." Had he led by the other, the Prussian Division
would have found it impassable by their Artillery.
The rain of the previous night had rendered the
ground extremely heavy; and in fact a mistake might
have changed the destiny of Europe.

I should have thought that every inch of ground in
the neighbourhood of Waterloo would have been
surveyed ; for it is well known that the Duke recon-
noitred the position the previous year; and had
previously determined where the fight would be for
the protection of Belgium.

TWO MEN have not been done justice to in the

history of the campaign : **Grouchy, and** Thielman. Napoleon, **who** invariably **blamed everybody** but himself, **insisted that Grouchy was a** traitor ; **and was paid.** A **more absurd fabrication never came even from his lips, who, as the Duke said,** "never tripped **into Truth."** Thanks **to the exertions, and admirable strategy of Thielman, Grouchy was** entirely **unable to make the attack on the Prussians which he, no** doubt, would otherwise have done. The **more** the matter is looked into, the more clearly will **this** appear. Thielman held Grouchy's Division in what might be called a "movable vice," the whole **day :** and **Grouchy could do nothing** more than he **did.**

I HAVE NEVER UNDERSTOOD **why the Officer Commanding in Chief the Cavalry should not** ride **with the Commander in Chief, as does** the General **Officer** commanding the Royal Artillery. I **should** have thought that such a system would be infinitely better than for the Commander in Chief, who is generally an Infantry Officer, to send **messages, which may or may** not be understood, **as at Balaclava, to the** Officer Commanding the Cavalry.

I HAVE **spoken of a conversation** between Napoleon

T

I. and Count Flahault, who was his companion in his flight from Waterloo to Charleroi. Count Flahault, who was on terms of personal intimacy with the Emperor, and his family, said to him "Is not your Majesty surprized?" Napoleon replied "No: it has been the same thing since Creçy;" throwing, as was his wont, the blame upon the brave soldiers who had died for him by thousands on that day.

A common friend asked me if he might inquire as to this fact from Count Flahault, when he was French Ambassador in London. I gave him permission to do so; and he reported to me subsequently that Count Flahault had said that it was true, word for word.

Napoleon's conduct towards Marshal Ney, his constant companion at arms, and, as Napoleon himself called him, 'the bravest of the brave,' was atrocious. Not only had Ney risked his life over and over again at Waterloo; not only had he headed the last desperate charge of the Old Guard, fighting, after his horse had been killed, on foot, and still holding his ground at the head of the Column, which received *twenty-nine rounds* of grape and canister shot, at *fifty yards* distance, before it began to yield; not only had he with difficulty, weary, and foot-sore, in the crowd of fugitives, scarcely survived the battle; but he had made for Napoleon a sacrifice greater than all this.

What was his reward? The Emperor lost not a moment in turning upon him; and endeavouring to throw the blame for the destruction of the French Army upon his ablest Lieutenant.

Contrast this conduct with that of Napoleon III. at Sedan.

Nothing would have been easier for the defeated Emperor than to have thrown the blame of such an overwhelming disaster upon his Generals, Macmahon or Wimpfen; he knew that the future of his Dynasty would be probably fatally affected by the admission that the responsibility of surrender rested upon him. He made no attempt to put the blame on other shoulders: he himself sent his personal aide-de-camp to hoist the flag of surrender on the citadel of Sedan. Whatever may have been the shortcomings of Napoleon III., he knew the meaning of the word 'Gentleman.'

NO MAN IN HIS ARMY was so much exposed during the battle as the Duke himself. He rode along the top of the ridge, now demolished, which sheltered his troops in some measure from the fire of the French Artillery. This was done, not in the slightest degree for theatrical display; but because, after carefully balancing in his mind the advantages, and disadvantages, he determined that it was better for him to do so. He felt that everything depended upon himself; and that the loss of his life might be the loss of his Army. On the other hand, he knew that he had to deal with troops, not, with a few exceptions, veterans; but chiefly boys, for they were hardly more, many of whom had never been engaged; and who had had no opportunity of seeing him win a battle. He felt that his first object must be to inspire confidence in his soldiers. His calmness of demeanour, his methodical way of dealing with the various Regiments during the day, all of which was visible to his men, gave them unbounded confidence in the success of his orders.

Not only did he feel this; but he also felt that he would show to the brave men who fought under him, that however great were their risks, however much he exacted from their courage, and their endurance, he exacted the same qualities, and conduct from himself. All that they risked he risked; at any moment their lives might have been sacrificed; so might his at any moment. There was not one, from the Chief of his

Staff to the last joined recruit, who did not know, and who did not see the self-sacrifice of this great man. Not a private in the ranks but felt during that tremendous conflict that the Duke of Wellington, the man of Wealth, Rank, and Success, with the World at his feet, was jeopardizing his life to at least the same degree as the poor outcast, who had become a soldier from starvation.

THERE MUST HOWEVER, have been a deeper feeling in Wellington's breast.

Those who have obtained extraordinary, and almost inordinate influence over mankind mainly by Military Genius have persuaded themselves that they were the instruments of the Almighty. We can hardly be surprized that Mahomet did so; and Attila called himself "The Scourge of God."

A Thought, the converse of this, must have visited the Duke. He knew that in those Belgian meadows he was fighting the true, honest cause of Civilization, and of Freedom. He had known his own long, and successful career. He knew that those opposed to him were fighting bravely for a man whom Honesty, and Honour had ceased to respect; and he felt, I can have no doubt, that the battle would be his.

Anxiety may have crossed his mind in the long delay of the arrival of his faithful allies; but he never doubted the result of the day : and he must have felt during the Greatest Battle that the World has ever known, that it was *his* guiding spirit that would give Europe half a century of peace.

Well might he say, with unaffected Piety, "THE FINGER OF PROVIDENCE WAS UPON ME."

THE BALL.

THERE was a sound of Revelry by night;
　　And Belgium's Capital had gather'd then
Her Beauty and her Chivalry; and bright
The lamps shone o'er fair women, and brave men:
A thousand hearts beat happily; and when
Music arose with its voluptuous swell,
Soft eyes look'd love to eyes which spake again;
And all went merry as a marriage-bell:
But Hush! Hark! a deep sound strikes like a rising
　　knell!

"Did ye not hear it?　No: 'twas but the wind;
Or the car rattling o'er the stony street:
On with the dance! let Joy be unconfined:
No sleep till morn, when Youth and Pleasure meet
To chase the glowing Hours with flying feet:
But, Hark! that heavy sound breaks in once more;
As if the clouds its echo would repeat;
And nearer, clearer, deadlier than before!
Arm! Arm! it is; it is; the Cannon's opening Roar!

LIBRARY
OF THE
UNIVERSITY
OF
CALIFORNIA

"Within a windowed niche of that High Hall
Sate Brunswick's fated chieftain; he did hear
That sound the first amidst the Festival;
And caught its tone with Death's prophetic ear:
And when they smiled, because he deem'd it near,
His heart more truly knew that peal too well,
Which stretch'd his father on a bloody bier;
And roused the Vengeance blood alone could quell:
He rush'd into the field, and, foremost fighting, fell.

"Ah! then, and there, was hurrying to and fro;
And gathering tears; and tremblings of distress;
And cheeks all pale, which but an hour ago
Blush'd at the praise of their own loveliness:
And there were sudden partings; such as press
The life from out young hearts; and choking sighs
Which ne'er might be repeated: Who could guess
If ever more should meet those mutual eyes;
Since upon Night so sweet such awful Morn could
     rise?

"And there was mounting in hot haste: the Steed,
The mustering Squadron, and the clattering car,
Went pouring forward with impetuous speed;
And swiftly forming in the ranks of War:

And the deep thunder, peal on peal, afar :

And near, the beat of the alarming drum

Roused up the soldier, ere the Morning Star :

While throng'd the Citizens with Terror dumb ;

Or whispering, with white lips, "The Foe ! They

    come ! they come ! "

"And Wild, and High, the "Cameron's Gathering"

    rose !

The War-note of Lochiel ; which Albyn's hills

Have heard ; and heard, too, have her Saxon foes :

How, in the noon of night, that Pibroch thrills,

Savage, and shrill ! But with the breath which fills

Their mountain-pipe, so fill the mountaineers

With the fierce native daring, which instils

The stirring memory of a thousand years :

And Evan's, Donald's, fame rings in each Clansman's

    ears !

"And Ardennes waves above them her green

    leaves,

Dewy with nature's tear-drops, as they pass ;

Grieving, if aught inanimate e'er grieves,

Over the unreturning brave ; Alas !

Ere evening to be trodden like the grass,
Which now beneath them, but above shall grow
In its next verdure ; when this fiery mass
Of living Valour, rolling on the Foe,
And burning with high Hope, shall moulder cold, and
    low.

" Last noon beheld them full of lusty life ;
Last eve in Beauty's circle proudly gay ;
The Midnight brought the signal-sound of strife ;
The Morn the marshalling in arms ; the Day
Battle's magnificently-stern array !
The thunder-clouds close o'er it : which when rent
The earth is cover'd thick with other clay ;
Which her own clay shall cover, heap'd, and pent,
Rider and horse ; friend, foe ; in one red burial
    blent ! "

IN THE SPRING of 1884, Colonel Montague, formerly commanding the 4th Hussars, asked me, at the Carlton Club, whether I could give him information relating to the Duchess of Richmond's ball ; which took place at Brussels on the 15th of June, 1815 ; the night before the battle of Quatre-Bras.

I told him that I would do my best to ascertain the

facts. Soon afterwards I happened to meet **Lord de Ros** at an evening party at Londonderry **House, Park Lane.** I mentioned the subject to him, and he reminded me that his mother, **Lady De Ros**, whom I had known all my life, would be glad to tell me all that she knew about the matter. I wrote to Lady de Ros; and immediately communicated her reply to Colonel Montague. The following letter has lately been handed to me by him. It bears the date, and post-mark of August 8, 1884.

"Dear Colonel Montague,

"I **trust** that illness has not kept you away from the Carlton: I received **last** night a very interesting letter on the **point anent** which **you asked me.**

"It is from **Lady de Ros, who was present at the ball**; and at whose father's house (**The Duke of Richmond's) it was given.** She says 'It was at our house, Rue de la Blanchisserie. The house *and street* no longer existed in 1869: the house stood in a garden in the lower part of the **town.** I have a plan of the ballroom; and a list of the invitations to the ball, which I will show you on my return to London.'

"The thermometer being at 90° in the shade while I write, you will understand how much I appreciate your interest in those glorious days.

"My father was on the Staff; as A.D.C. to the Commander of the Cavalry : and my cousin, Captain Thomas Craufurd of the Third Guards was the only Officer killed in the kitchen-garden of *Gomont*.

"Yours very truly,

"WILLIAM FRASER.

"Lt Col. Montague."

I subsequently saw Lady de Ros; and had a very interesting conversation with her on the subject. She was so good as to give me the list of those invited to the Ball; which I append. She gave me many particulars as regards what happened at the ball; the dancing continuing all night after the departure of the Officers; not by the ladies of the house, but by other young ladies, in a more or less heartless way. Lady de Ros informed me that when she and the late Lord de Ros had endeavoured to find the place some years ago (it appears it was in 1868), they completely failed : that they were informed that not only the house, but *the street*, in fact the whole " quartier " had been demolished ; and that the quest of the ball-room was perfectly hopeless. Lady de Ros produced a plan on a large scale ; but as she told me that the Duke of Richmond's house no longer existed, I scarcely glanced at it; and retain no impression

whatever of what it was like. Colonel Montague, I
may mention, had on two occasions done his utmost
to find the ball-room; but he, like Lady de Ros, had
failed; and for the same reason: they both accepted
as true what they were told. Lady de Ros told me
that the Ball was in a long narrow room, that had at
one time been a coachmaker's depôt: and was used
occasionally by her sisters and herself, as a play-room.

The following is the List of Invitations to the
Duchess of Richmond's Ball at Brussels, June 15,
1815.

H.R.H. the Prince of Orange.

H.R.H. Prince Frederic of Orange.

H.R.H. the Duke of Brunswick.

Prince of Nassau.

Duc d'Arenberg.

Prince Auguste d'Arenberg.

Prince Pierre d'Arenberg.

Le Maire de Bruxelles.

Duc et Duchesse de Beaufort et Mademoiselle.

Duc et Duchesse D'Ursel.

Marquis et Marquise D'Assche [from their house we
saw the wounded brought in: Lord Uxbridge, Lord
F. Somerset, &c.].

Comte et Comtesse D'Oultremont.

Comtesse Douairière D'Oultremont et les Mesde-
moiselles.

Comte et Comtesse Liedekerke Beaufort.

Comte et Comtesse Auguste Liedekerke et Mademoiselle.

Comte et Comtesse Latour Lupin.

Comte et Comtesse Mercy D'Argenteau.

Comte et Comtesse de Grasiac.

Comtesse de Luiny.

Comtesse de Ruilly.

Baron et Baronne D'Hooghvoorst.

Mademoiselle D'Hooghvoorst et Monsieur C.
D'Hooghvoorst.

Madame Constant D'Hooghvoorst.

Monsieur et Madame Vander Capellan.

Baron de Herelt.

Baron de Tuybe.

Baron Brockhausen.

General Baron Vincent, wounded at Waterloo.

General Pozzo di Borgo.

General Alava.

Comte de Belgade.

Comte de la Rochefoucauld.

Gen. D'Oudenarde.

Col. Knife, (?) A.D.C.

Col. Ducayla.

Major Ronnchenberg, A.D.C.

Col. Tripp, A.D.C.

Capt. de Lubeck, A.D.C. to H.R.H. the Duke of Brunswick.

Earl and Countess of Conyngham, and Lady Elizabeth Conyngham.

Viscount Mount Charles and Hon. Mr Conyngham (afterwards 2nd Marquess Conyngham).

Countess Mount Norris and Lady Juliana Annesley.

Countess Dowager of Waldegrave.

Duke of Wellington.

Lord and Lady Fitzroy Somerset (neither were present; Lord Fitzroy lost his arm at Waterloo).

Lord and Lady John Somerset.

M^r and Lady Frances Webster.

M^r and Lady Caroline Capel and Miss Capel.

Lord and Lady George Seymour and Miss Seymour.

M^r and Lady Charlotte Greville.

Viscountess Hawarden.

Sir Henry and Lady Susan Clinton (he was Lt-Gen. and G.C.B. and commanded a Division).

Lady Alvanley and the Miss Ardens.

Sir James, Lady, and Miss Craufurd.

Sir George Berkeley, K.C.B., and Lady Berkeley.

Lady and Miss Sutton.

Sir Sidney and Lady Smith, and Miss Rumbolds.

Sir William and Lady Johnstone.

Sir Hew and Lady Dalrymple.

Sir William and Lady Delancy.

Hon. Mrs Pole (afterwards Lady Maryborough).

M^r, M^rs, and Miss Lance, and Mr. Lance, jun.

M^r and the Miss Ords.

M^r and Mrs Greathed.

M^r and Mrs Lloyd.

Hon. Sir Charles Stuart, G.C.B. (Minister at Bruxelles),
and Mr Stuart.

Earl of Uxbridge (commanded the Cavalry; lost his
leg at Waterloo).

Earl of Portarlington.

Earl of March, A.D.C. to H.R.H. the Prince of
Orange.

Gen. Lord Edward Somerset (commanded a Brigade
of Cavalry; wounded at Waterloo).

Lord Charles FitzRoy.

Lord Robert Manners.

Lt-Gen. Lord Hill (commanding the 2nd Corps).

Lord Rendlesham.

Lord Hay, A.D.C. (killed at Quatre-Bras).

Lord Saltoun.

Lord Apsley (afterwards Earl Bathurst).

Hon. Col. Stanhope (Guards).

Hon. Col. Abercromby (Guards ; wounded).

Hon. Col. Ponsonby, afterwards Sir Frederick Ponsonby, K.C.B. (severely wounded).

Hon. Col. Acheson (Guards).

Hon. Col. Stewart.

Hon. Mr O. Bridgeman, A.D.C. to Lord Hill.

Hon. Mr Percival.

Hon. Mr Stopford.

Hon. Mr John Gordon.

Hon. Mr Edgecombe.

Hon. Mr Seymour Bathurst, A.D.C. to Gen. Maitland.

Hon. Mr Forbes.

Hon. Mr Hastings Forbes.

Hon. Major Dawson.

Hon. Mr Dawson, 18th Light Dragoons.

Maj.-Gen. Sir Hussey Vivian (commanded a Brigade of Cavalry).

Mr. Horace Seymour, A.D.C. (afterwards Sir Horace Seymour, K.C.B.).

Col. Hervey, A.D.C. (afterwards Sir Felton Hervey, Bart.).

Col. Fremantle, A.D.C.

Lord George Lennox, A.D.C.

Lord Arthur Hill, A.D.C. (afterwards Gen. Lord Sandys).

Hon. Major Percy, A.D.C. (son of 1ˢᵗ Earl of Beverley. He brought home three Eagles and dispatches).

Hon. Mʳ Cathcart, A.D.C. (afterwards Sir George Cathcart; killed at Inkerman, 1854).

Hon. Sir Alexander Gordon, A.D.C. (died of his wounds at Waterloo).

Sir Colin Campbell, K.C.B., A.D.C.

Sir John Byng, G.C.B. (created Earl of Strafford; commanded 2ⁿᵈ Brigade of Guards).

Lᵗ-Gen. Sir John Elley, K.C.B.

Sir George Scovell, K.C.B. (Major commanding Staff Corps of Cavalry).

Sir George Wood, Col. R.A.

Sir Henry Bradford.

Sir Robert Hill, Kᵗ }
Sir Noel Hill, K.C.B. } (Brothers of Lord Hill.)

Sir William Ponsonby, K.C.B. (brother of Lord Ponsonby; commanded a Brigade of Cavalry; killed at Waterloo).

Sir Andrew Barnard (afterwards Governor of Chelsea Hospital).

Sir Denis Pack, Maj.-Gen., G.C.B. (commanded a Brigade).

Sir James Kemp, Maj.-Gen., G.C.B. (commanded a Brigade).

Sir Pulteney Malcolm.

Sir Thomas Picton, Lt-Gen. (commanded 5th Division; killed at Waterloo).

Maj.-Gen. Sir Edward Barnes, Adjt.-Gen. (wounded at Waterloo).

Sir James Gambier.

Hon. General Dundas.

Lt-Gen. Cooke (commanded 1st Division).

Maj.-Gen. Maitland (afterwards Sir Peregrine, G.C.B.; commanded 1st Brigade of Guards).

Maj.-Gen. Adam (not present; commanded a Brigade; afterwards Sir Frederick Adam, K.C.B.).

Col. Washington.

Col. Woodford (afterwards F.M. Sir Alexander Woodford, G.C.B., Governor of Chelsea).

Col. Rowan, 52nd (afterwards Sir Charles Rowan, Chief Commissioner of Police).

Col. Wyndham (afterwards Gen. Sir Henry Wyndham).

Col. Cumming, 18th Light Dragoons.

Col. Bowater (afterwards Gen. Sir Edward Bowater).

Col. Torrens (afterwards Adjt.-Gen. in India).

Col. Fuller.

Col. Dick, 42nd (killed at Sobraon, 1846).

Col. Cameron, 92nd (killed at Quatre-Bras).

Col. Barclay, A.D.C. to the Duke of York.

Col. Hill (?) (Col. Clement Hill, brother to Lord Hill).

Major Gunthorpe, A.D.C. to Gen. Maitland.

Major Churchill, A.D.C. to Lord Hill and Q.M.G. (killed in India).

Major Hamilton, A.D.C. to Gen. Sir E. Barnes.

Major Harris, Brigade Major to Sir Hussey Vivian (lost an arm).

Major Hunter Blair (wounded).

Capt. Mackworth, A.D.C. to Lord Hill.

Capt. Keane, A.D.C. to Sir Hussey Vivian.

Capt. FitzRoy.

Capt. Wildman, 7th Hussars, A.D.C. to Lord Uxbridge.

Capt. Fraser, 7th Hussars (afterwards Sir James Fraser, Bart.).

Capt. Verner, 7th Hussars.

Capt. Elphinstone, 7th Hussars (taken prisoner June 17).

Capt. Webster.

Capt. Somerset, A.D.C. to Gen. Lord Edward Somerset.

Capt. Yorke, A.D.C. to Gen. Adam (afterwards Sir Charles Yorke; not present).

Capt. Gore, A.D.C. to Sir James Kempt.

Capt. Pakenham, R.A.

Capt. Dumaresq, A.D.C. to Gen. Sir John Byng (died of wounds).

Capt. Dawkins, A.D.C.

Capt. Disbrowe, **A.D.C. to Gen.** Sir G. Cook.

Capt. Bowles, Coldstream Guards (afterwards Gen. Sir George Bowles, **Lieutenant of the Tower).**

Capt. Hesketh, Grenadier Guards.

Capt. Gurwood (afterwards Col. Gurwood).

Capt. Allix, Grenadier Guards.

Mr Russell, A.D.C.

Mr Brooke, 12th Dragoon Guards.

Mr Huntley, 12th Dragoon Guards.

Mr Lionel Hervey (in diplomacy).

Mr Leigh.

Mr Shakespear, 18th.

M^r O'Grady, 7th Hussars (afterwards **Lord Guillamore).**

Mr Smith, 95th, Brigadier-Major to Sir Denis Packe (killed at Waterloo).

Mr Fludyer, Scots Fusilier Guards.

2 Mr Montagus (John, and Henry, late Lord
Rokeby, G.C.B.).

Mr A. Greville.

Mr Baird.

Mr Robinson, 32nd.

Mr James.

Mr Chad.

Mr Dawkins.

Dr Hyde.

Mr Hume.

Rev. Mr Brixall.

ON MY RETURN to Brussels from Waterloo last
August I visited the old Cemetery; in a neglected
corner of which were buried the bodies of the Officers
who died in Brussels from wounds received in the
Battles of the 15th, 16th, and 17th of June. Some of
the graves are empty; the bodies having been removed
to England. Over a few the stones still remain: the
only name that I could recognize as being distinguished
was that of Sir William de Lancy, the Deputy-Quarter-
master General; whose death while speaking to the
Duke I have described.

I subsequently paid a visit to Count ——, a
Belgian Nobleman, well-known in the world of Art.

I told the Count that I was very anxious to find, if possible, the scene of the famous ball. I mentioned to him that in Cotton's "Voice from Waterloo" it is stated that the Duke of Richmond's house was in the Rue des Cendres; whereas a lady, who had been present, had more than once told me that it was in the Rue de la Blanchisserie.

The Count said "That may well be; for the Rue des Cendres, and the Rue de la Blanchisserie are back to back." This first gave me hopes. I went straight from his house to the Rue de la Blanchisserie; and examined the first section of it, if I may use the term, very carefully. I could find no house that answered the description in any way whatever. I then walked up the Rue des Cendres to the left. On my right hand I noticed a vast Hospital; with an extensive dead wall. A gentleman standing in his doorway answered my questions by telling me that the Duke of Richmond's house had been *absorbed;* and made part of this large Hospital. I rang the bell; and was immediately admitted by one of the Nursing Sisters of the Order of St Augustin. I at once asked her if she would point out to me the Duke of Richmond's house; or, at least, what remained of it. Passing from the "porte cochère," in which we were standing, she at once pointed to a house on the left, which she said was the Duke of Richmond's house. Adding "It is now, as you see, part of the Hospital; I cannot allow you to enter; for it is the abode of the Nursing Sisters."

The windows were wide open, the weather being very hot; and I could distinctly examine the rooms from outside. The ceilings were ornamental, in the Renaissance style; the central ornament of one had been painted black, and the other was still gilded : it was obvious that the rooms had not been built for the purposes of a Hospital; they had evidently been the dwelling-rooms of a family of good position. Between the rooms were *steps leading into the court-yard, or old garden, in which we were standing.* My first impulse naturally was to examine the rooms so carefully, and accurately as I could; *hoping that one of them might be the famous ball-room :* but neither of them was nearly large enough. They were the ordinary sitting-rooms of a family; and *neither of them could have held the two hundred and twenty persons ;* which was the number of guests according to the list given to me by Lady de Ros. I looked round the yard, which I have named; and was leaving the premises in despair. I said to the Nursing Sister

"Would you allow me to go back by myself, and think for a few minutes?" I felt that being so near the quest, and not to find it, was provoking. I stood in the yard; and carefully examined the adjacent buildings. In the plan which I reproduce, a facsimile of that lately published by Lady de Ros, none of the buildings adjacent to the Duke of Richmond's house are given. The whole of the buildings of the Rue de la Blanchisserie are omitted : it is the ground floor of the Duke's house only; and no more represents the locality than the ground-plan of Lord Sefton's house would represent Belgrave Square. I, at length, noticed behind me a lofty wall; and over the top of this I observed a gabled roof. I had no idea that the Rue de la Blanchisserie did not terminate at the foot of the Rue des Cendres; but on asking the Nursing Sister what that building was behind the lofty wall of separation, she at once said "That is the great Brewery of the Rue de la Blanchisserie." I replied "But surely the Rue de la B. stops below?" "No," she said, "it continues." My hopes were raised.

I walked down the Rue des Cendres, turned to the left, into the continuation of the Rue de la Blanchisserie, which is obviously an old street, much older than the Rue des Cendres; and rang the bell at number 40. I was admitted; and what took place will be found in my letter to "The Times," p. 299.

I measured the room by paces; and may have slightly overstated its length; and diminished its height. There were doors at either end; which had at one time communicated with the court-yard of the Duke of Richmond's house. It is clear that the lofty wall, separating the hospital yard from the granary, was built long after the latter: it blocks the lights completely on that side. Returning to my hotel, and believing that the one person in the world who would be most delighted at the discovery, was Lady de Ros; although the weather was very hot, and Brussels stifling, I wrote her a letter, sketching briefly what I had found; not asking a single question; for I had no more doubt at that time than I have now that this was the room in which the Ball was given; but mentioning particulars which I thought would interest her. I wrote to no one else. I was delighted to think that I should please Lady de Ros; and this feeling I expressed in the strongest terms. A day or two afterwards I wrote to Colonel Montague to the same effect: leaving Brussels, and travelling leisurely into Germany, I wrote from Homburg my first letter addressed to the Editor of "The Times." On the same day on which I saw "The Times" containing my letter, I received a note from Lady de Ros, who had read it.

Before leaving Homburg Sir Albert Rollit, and the Rev. Teignmouth Shore, separately volunteered the information which, at different times, they had received from Lord William Lennox.

MY LETTER appeared in "THE TIMES" of August 25.

THE WATERLOO BALL.

To the Editor of The Times.

SIR,—The following particulars relating to a frequently disputed question may interest your readers. A few days ago I visited the field of Waterloo. The only alteration observable is the improved condition of the farm-houses, historically famous, of Gomont, popularly known as Hougoumont; and of 'La Haye Sainte.' I regretted to find, in the former, that the monumental stone placed on the spot where Captain Thomas Craufurd, of the 3rd Guards, fell had disappeared. I hope that it may be replaced.

On the road between 'La Belle Alliance,' and Genappe I was courteously permitted to see the room in which Napoleon slept the night before Waterloo; the tables upon which he spread his maps on the morning of the 18th of June; and the spot, in the garden, from which he had his first view of the Field of Battle.

At Genappe I saw the ground on which the 1st Life Guards successfully charged the French Lancers, on the 17th of June; and, a few miles further on, the field of Quatre Bras, the scene of almost, if not quite, the sharpest fight of the British Army, appeared picturesque in the light of a setting sun. A monument is, I am glad to say, soon to be placed on the spot, close to the Nivelles road, where the heroic Duke of Brunswick "fell as his father fell"; at the head of his devoted corps.

One pathetic incident of this battle has escaped the notice of Poets, and Painters. I can remember my father saying that on the evening of Quatre Bras he noticed many Officers lying dead in the silk stockings, and buckled shoes which they had worn at the Duchess of Richmond's ball on the previous night; their servants having joined the column earlier making it impossible for them to change their full-dress uniforms.

On returning to Brussels, I determined to find, if

possible, the scene of the Ball given by the Duchess
of Richmond, the evening before Quatre Bras.

Endless have been the discussions, angry the
quarrels relating to the locality of this ball. Brussels
during that brief, but momentous Campaign has been
described by the mighty spirits of the century. Byron,
Thackeray, and Scott were inspired in the highest
degree by the circumstances of that time. "Childe
Harold," "Vanity Fair," and "Paul's Letters to his
Kinsfolk" will live as Classics of the English language.
The discovery of the scene immortalized by these
writers seemed to me worthy of the effort.

I am glad to say that I succeeded.

Some time before leaving England I conversed with
a lady who danced with my father at the ball [this is
doubtful], and who has, as you will see from her name,
which I enclose, the best means of knowing where it
took place. This lady, giving me at the same time a
list of those who were invited, told me that Lord
Byron's allusion to "that high hall" was "nonsense."
She added that the ball took place, not in the Duke of
Richmond's house, but in a coachmaker's depôt, a low-
roofed room, at the rear of it; the street being named
Rue de la Blanchisserie. I made many inquiries in
England, and in Brussels. No one knew anything of

the place; but all agreed that the scene of the ball had been frequently sought without success : and that it no longer existed.

I at last ascertained that the site of the Duke of Richmond's house was now covered by a large Hospital in the Rue des Cendres. I visited the Hospital, and one of the Nursing Sisters politely pointed out a wing which had formed part of the Duke's house. I examined the garden behind this wing ; neither in this nor in the building itself was there any trace of a ball-room. I observed above the wall of the Hospital the roof of a high building ; and inquired what it was ; the sister replied that it was the Brewery of the Rue de la Blanchisserie. I walked round to this street ; and was informed by the proprietor of the brewery that he knew nothing on the subject. After some conversation I asked if he could tell me of whom his father purchased the property; he replied of a coachbuilder named Van Asch. I inquired if the coachbuilder had a depôt. "Yes, a very large one ; it is now my granary." He then took me to the first floor (entresol), and I found myself in the room, the remembrance of which will live so long as the English language. It is 120 ft. long, 54 ft. broad, and about 13 ft. high, the floor smooth enough to be danced on to-night. This room answers precisely to the description given to me: it is immediately in the rear of the Duke of Richmond's house: it is in the street named: it belonged in 1815 to a coachbuilder: and it is capable of holding at least 400 persons.

I do not think that further proof can be required. I have the permission of the proprietor to give his name; V. Vanginderachter, Brasseur, Rue de la Blanchisserie, 40 et 42. He most courteously added that he would be glad to show the room to visitors.

Your obedient servant,

Homburg. WILLIAM FRASER.

THE FOLLOWING Leading Article appeared in "THE MORNING POST" on the 27th of August, 1888.

"THERE is, probably, no merely Social Event in the History of the present century which has become more enshrined in the public memory than the Ball given by the Duchess of Richmond at Brussels on the eve of the Battle of Quatre Bras; which immediately preceded Waterloo. Romance, and Literature have vied with each other in the endeavour to depict a scene so brilliant in its beginning, so stirring in its development, and so darkened with the shadow of the coming events, which was thrown beforehand on

its closing hours. But of the great mass of com-
petitors who have striven to identify their names with
the story of this historic night two, and these two
appropriately enough Englishmen, have outstripped
all others. The verse of Byron, and the prose of
Thackeray, have procured for the Brussels ball a
place in the classical literature of England which will
preserve the recollection of it for all time. Strangely
enough, in an age distinguished for relic hunting of
every description, the almost universal curiosity to
stand 'Within a windowed niche of that high hall'
has been invariably baffled by the accident that nobody seemed quite sure where the house occupied by
the Duke of Richmond was to be found. The secret
has, to all appearances, been finally discovered by
Sir William Fraser. A lady, whose competence to
relate the facts is absolutely vouched for, still survives
as a representative of the 'Beauty, and Chivalry'
gathered in Belgium's capital, and by her directions
Sir William Fraser was enabled to track the spot
which henceforward will invest Brussels with a new
attraction for the British and American tourist. The
Ball, according to this veteran participator in it, took
place not in the Duke's house, but 'in a coachmaker's
depôt, a long, low-roofed room at the back of it ; the

street being named the Rue de la Blanchisserie.'
Here at once may be discovered an adequate reason
for previous failures to identify the spot. The land
once occupied by the Duke of Richmond's house is
now covered by a Hospital looking upon the Rue des
Cendres. The coachmaker's depôt is now the
granary of a Brewery, and still stands back to back
with the Hospital, but not, as before, connected with
it. Thus, even if there had been no doubt about
which was really the house, there would have been
no possibility, in face of the local rearrangements, for
discovering the long-lost ball-room. It is this fact
probably that accounts for the preference assigned to
many other houses in Brussels which possessed rooms
corresponding more to the 'high hall' where 'Brunswick's fated chieftain' first heard the roar of the
French cannon with a prophetic instinct that his
father's fate at Jena would be his on the morrow of
Quatre Bras. Byron, in the opinion of the lady who
had the advantage of being there, 'talked nonsense'
in describing as a 'high hall' this low room of about
thirteen feet in height. Considering, however, that
the poetic inspiration was in this case wholly dependent on imagination, it would be somewhat hard to
blame the poet himself for picturing the ducal hos-

pitalities in language which probably slipped naturally
from his pen. Whether the room was thirteen feet
high or thirty, it is sacred ground to more people
even than the large class who rejoice to sit in the
favourite tavern seats of Johnson, or walk up the
steps of some house where one of Dickens's fictional
characters is represented as living.

" For the granary in the Rue de la Blanchisserie has
a great advantage over the famous places of Fiction
which can be claimed only by the few spots where
truths which are even more strange have been
enacted. At least half that brilliant assembly must
have trembled for what the morrow would bring forth ;
while for the Duke of Wellington, and his officers, the
night was one of intense anxiety and of high-strung
anticipation of the possible fate of Europe. Many
ridiculous stories were current at the time, and are
credited even now, of the circumstances under which
Wellington first discovered the rapid and decisive
movements of his great antagonist. The real facts,
however, were soon afterwards made clear in a
history of Napoleon, which was published for the
' Family Library.' Wellington had been informed
by his scouts of the French advance before the
ball began ; and at first it was decided to counter-

mand the permission to attend it. Motives of policy, however, decided the Commander-in-Chief to keep his information to himself. The inhabitants of Brussels were trembling for the fate of themselves, and their beautiful city; and even throughout the eventful days which followed readily believed every rumour to the effect that the British troops were cut to pieces, and that the French were advancing to sack the capital. Moreover, the spirit of the foreign levies was broken by the exploits which had made the armies of Napoleon seem well nigh invincible; and much might be lost by prematurely exciting them. Accordingly, Wellington bid his General Officers go to the ball; and after ten o'clock to steal away one by one in preparation for the march. Thus it happened that the tragic interest of this festival has taken so deep a hold upon the imagination. From Picton to young Frederick Howard, immortalized by Byron, the English officers quitted their partners, in many cases to be heard of again only when, like the unworthy George Osborne of 'Vanity Fair,' they were lying on the field of battle dead, with a bullet through their hearts.

"There is little wonder that this veritable 'dance of death' should have appealed to the Genius of Poets,

and prose-writers alike. Admitting the justice of
Johnson's aphorism that 'where Truth is sufficient to
fill the mind, Fiction is worse than useless' the palm
must in this instance be awarded to Byron. The
graphic account of Thackeray can scarcely be surpassed by anyone who is daring enough to essay the
task of touching the subject. Nevertheless, the days of
Waterloo seem still too near for the present generation
quite to accept the intrusion of such characters as
Becky Sharp, and Osborne upon the stage of these
stern, and saddening realities. Paradoxically enough,
and in spite of the 'high hall,' it is the Poet who has
adhered to Truth, and the gifted novelist who has
mixed it with fiction. 'I am not sure,' said Sir
Walter Scott, always the more generous of Byron's
contemporary critics, 'that any verses in our language
surpass in Vigour, and in Feeling this most beautiful
description.' This verdict has, we believe, been
fully endorsed by posterity; which recognizes in the
lines of Byron just that aid which the art of the Poet
could lend to the march of facts at once so stately
and so terrible. The courteous proprietor of the
'long, low-roofed room,' who has declared his willingness to throw it open for public inspection, is likely
to find the number of his visitors truly considerable.

The placid fields of Waterloo afford very little evidence to the pilgrims of history of the the dire event which has made them Immortal. The land of waving corn, and 'reckless birds' is suggestive now, as it was to Byron, principally of 'what it cannot bring.' But in the old granary of the Rue de la Blanchisserie the lovers of the scenes which have become historic may well feel that the echoes of the past have become audible once more."

ON THE SAME DAY "THE DAILY TELEGRAPH" commented on my letter as follows :

" ' Everything,' says the proverb, 'comes to those who know how to wait'; although the sage monition was once met by a scoffer with the irreverent rejoinder that the things most earnestly desiderated were often so late in coming that life was not long enough to wait for their advent. Historical students, however, if they be worthy of the task which they have set themselves, are bound to be of a more patient temperament; and they may account it a comparatively trifling matter if they have only had to wait some three-and-seventy years before having reason to be grateful to Sir William Fraser for the discovery of the exact locality of the historic enter-

tainment given by the Duchess of Richmond, at
Brussels, the night before Quatre Bras ; and popularly
known as the ' Waterloo Ball.'   Sir William has been
rambling about the field of the 'King-making Victory' ;
and, after visiting Hougoumont, Genappe, and Quatre
Bras itself, he remembered that his father, who fought
gallantly in the campaign, had noticed on the last-
named battle-ground many British officers lying dead
in the silk stockings, and buckled shoes, which they
had worn at the Duchess's ball on the previous night ;
their servants having joined the columns earlier ; and
so making it impossible for their masters to change
their full-dress uniforms.   Moreover, before the
Baronet left England he had the advantage of con-
versing with a lady who had danced with his father at
this selfsame ball, and who was good enough inci-
dentally to remark that Lord Byron's allusion, in the
immortal lines in 'Childe Harold,' to 'that high
hall' was 'nonsense.'   The lady was apparently un-
aware that there is such a thing as poetic licence.
However, she added that the ball really took place in
a coachbuilder's shop, which happened to be a room
with a somewhat low roof, at the rear of the mansion
occupied by the Duke and Duchess of Richmond
during their sojourn in the Belgian capital ; the name

of the thoroughfare in which it was situated being the
Rue de la Blanchisserie. Sir William made many
inquiries on the subject both in England and abroad;
but all he could glean was that the precise scene of
the ball had often been sought for; though without
success.

"At length the researches of Sir William Fraser have
been rewarded. During his recent visit he ascertained
that the site of the Duke of Richmond's temporary
domicile at Brussels was now covered by a large
Hospital in the Rue des Cendres; one of the wings of
which is the original fabric; but neither here, nor in
the garden beyond, was there any trace of a ball-room.
The indefatigable Baronet, determined not to be
baffled, pursued his investigations until he observed,
beyond the hospital wall, the roof of a high building,
which he was informed was the brewery of the Rue
de la Blanchisserie. He walked round to the 'brasserie' in question; but the proprietor could tell him
nothing about any terpsichorean doings there in the
year 1815. His father, he said, had purchased the
property of a coachbuilder named Van Asch, and
his depôt for carriages was now his, the brewer's,
granary. This room he courteously offered to show
to his visitor; who was conducted to an apartment a

hundred and twenty feet long, fifty-four feet broad, and about thirteen feet high, the floor being quite smooth enough, even after this long lapse of time, to be danced upon. On the night of the 15th of June, 1815, the 'parquet' was, in all probability, chalked in a symmetrical and particoloured pattern. Certainly a saloon the altitude of which did not exceed that of two ordinarily strapping Life Guardsmen could not with technical precision be called a 'high hall'; but the Poet is King; and may consider himself to be as much above a mere question of inches as the German Emperor asserted that he was above grammar. It would, however, have been some slight consolation to the lovers of Byron had Sir William Fraser only been kind enough to tell us whether in this low-roofed ex-coachmaker's depôt there was anything in the nature of a 'windowed niche' suitable for the accommodation of 'Brunswick's fated chieftain,' who, by the way, did not, as Sir William Fraser seems to think, precisely fall 'as his father fell.' The old Duke of Brunswick, whose madly wicked proclamation led to the murder of Louis XVI. and half the horrors of the French Revolution, was not killed at the Battle of Jena. He was badly wounded there, but died at Dantzic some days afterwards. In any case, Sir William Fraser seems to have conclusively made out his contention that the 'Waterloo Ball' was held in the carriage depôt of the coachbuilder Van Asch; now the granary of the 'brasserie' Van-ginderachter, Nos. 40 and 42, Rue de la Blanchis-serie, Brussels; and the public are indebted to the Baronet for a long-needed, and vainly-sought-for piece of information. The doubt which for so many years has enveloped the question is not, after all, so very incomprehensible. The coachbuilder's ware-house was evidently used as an 'annexe' to the Duke of Richmond's house; and, considering that there were some four hundred guests at the ball, most of whom may have been almost strangers to their noble host and hostess, it is quite feasible that the majority of the company never troubled their heads for a moment whether the capacious, but low-roofed, ball-room was part and parcel of the house of their enter-tainers, or whether it belonged to some contiguous premises, of which opportunity had been taken, just as the promoters of the tea-party to Messrs. Smith O'Brien, and Meagher in 1848, 'by the Shannon Shore,' 'took the opportunity of Tim Doolan's store.' It was enough for the guests at the Duchess's ball that 'there was a sound of revelry by night,' that 'the

lamps shone o'er fair women and brave men,' that 'a
thousand hearts beat happily,' and that 'all went
merry as a marriage bell,' when a sound arose which
was not that of the wind nor of the car rattling o'er
the stony street, but 'the cannon's opening roar.'   It
does not in the least detract from the melody, and
majesty of Byron's stanzas, of which Walter Scott
wrote, 'I am not sure that any verses in our language
surpass in vigour and in feeling this most beautiful
description'—an opinion amply confirmed by Jeffrey,
who declares that 'there can be no finer proof of the
greatness of Byron's genius than the spirit and interest which he has contrived to communicate to his
picture of the often-drawn and difficult scene of the
breaking up from Brussels before the great battle'—
that early in the afternoon of the 15th a memorandum
from the Quartermaster-General's Department had
warned the Commanding Officers of Regiments of the
First Division to collect that night at Ath, and to be
in readiness to move at a moment's notice ; and that
at ten in the evening, when the ball had probably
begun, an 'after order,' signed by the Duke of Wellington himself, was issued deciding the immediate
march of the troops.   It was the Duke's wish, however, that all officers of rank should attend the ball,

to prevent any **panic which** might arise from **their** absence.

"The late Lord William **Pitt Lennox was, as a** young subaltern, on **the personal staff of the Duke in** the Waterloo **campaign, and in his novel of 'Percy Hamilton,' which is mainly autobiographical, he states that his Chief and his Etat-Major, of whom Lord William was one, took leave of the noble host and** hostess shortly after eleven o'clock; and, 'having changed their dress-clothes,' rode away to the front. The officers whom Sir William Fraser's father saw lying dead on the field of **Quatre Bras, '**in silk stockings, **and buckled shoes,' must have been Regimental Officers who were not so fortunate as the staff in being able to change their dress before joining their divisions.** The venerable and happily living **Earl** of Albemarle **was, as Ensign or Lieutenant** Kepp, at Waterloo. **It would be** curious to know whether the patriarchal veteran was at the 'Waterloo Ball'; and whether he went thither in silk stockings and buckled **shoes; a** garb which **for a** subaltern in **a marching regiment** in front **of** the enemy **would** have been manifestly **out of place.** They **used, however, to** order things **differently in the Navy; and there is on record a very characteristic** conversation between

Lord Collingwood and one of his flag captains on the advantages of going into battle in silken hose; the brusque 'Coll' expressing his opinion that, if an officer fought in silk stockings, and happened to get knocked over, his silken-clad extremities might save the surgeon much trouble if the amputation of one or both legs was required. No wonder if the valiant sea-lions who could talk thus placidly of the chances of death, and mutilation were the men of the 1ˢᵗ of June, and Cape Sᵗ Vincent, of the Nile, and Trafalgar. But in the Waterloo week it rained heavily; and the heroes who laid down their lives on the field of the great battle would have fought more comfortably in breeches and gaiters; or even in those trousers which Wellington had introduced for the use of his troops in the Peninsula; although he himself adhered to buckskins, and hessians. It is still possible that he might have worn kerseymeres, silk continuations, and buckled shoes at the ball in the Rue de la Blanchisserie; but there is one other point touching this memorable festival which, could Sir William Fraser clear it up, would entitle him to a still greater meed of gratitude at the hands of his contemporaries. Napoleon's travelling carriage, captured by the Prussians after Waterloo, and now at Madame Tussaud's, was built at Brussels. Was it built by Van Asch, who seemingly was a leading 'carrossier' of the period? The question is worth asking; for when Byron, after his separation from his wife, started on that which was virtually Childe Harold's Pilgrimage, he purchased at Brussels a travelling carriage which was the exact counterpart of the one made for Napoleon the Great. If Mynheer Van Asch was the maker, the Poet in all probability visited the depôt in the Rue de la Blanchisserie, which only recently had been used as a ball-room; and in that long, low apartment, converted by poetic licence into a 'high hall,' he might have felt the first inspiration for one of the most magnificent of his lyrical achievements."

I NEED NOT SAY that, reposing on a chair on the terrace of the Kur Saal of Homburg, I read these articles with complacency: reflections on the calm good sense, extensive reading, and judicial capacity of the writers followed: and I may have eaten my dinner at the excellent table d'hôte of the Hotel Victoria with increased zest on that day: but

> " What is mortal Happiness in truth?
> The torrent's smoothness ere it dash below ! "

The very next morning a friend "called my attention" to a contradiction on the part of Lady de Ros
to my carefully drawn conclusion.

The article did not give the terms used: but I
fairly assumed that they were the same as those
in Lady de Ros's letter to me: accordingly I wrote
the following letter, which appeared in "THE DAILY
TELEGRAPH" on the 5th of September.

THE WATERLOO BALL.

TO THE EDITOR OF THE DAILY TELEGRAPH.

SIR,—I read your article of the 28th ult. with surprize. The only note that I have received from Lady
de Ros was written after reading my published letter;
and is strongly confirmatory of my statement. You
will, perhaps, permit me to say, so briefly and so
clearly as I can, what has taken place.

Two [this should be four] years ago I received
from Lady de Ros the facts that the ball given by
her father and mother (the Duke and Duchess of
Richmond) the night before Quatre-Bras did not
take place in their house; but in a coachmaker's
depôt adjacent to it; and that this coachmaker's
depôt was in the Rue de la Blanchisserie. This
statement was given to me, not only verbally; but
subsequently in writing. Lady de Ros added that

Lord de Ros, and herself had tried hard, twenty years earlier, to find the room; and had failed; all those whom they consulted at Brussels having told them that the ball-room no longer existed. The house having disappeared, that the ball-room had gone with it was a natural conclusion. A friend of mine, a Colonel in the army, to whom I gave the facts, tried hard to find the room. He wrote to me from Brussels; and said that his inquiries were met with the invariable reply, "Ah, Monsieur, cela n'existe plus."

Having six near relations at the ball; and far more on public grounds; being at Brussels a few weeks ago, I determined to ascertain for myself whether this most memorable spot still remained. Of this I have now not the slightest doubt. I, like Lady de Ros, was told by all of whom I inquired that the ball-room was gone. One old gentleman assured me that the whole quarter had been demolished; and that there was no longer a Rue de la Blanchisserie.

I ascertained that the Duke of Richmond's house in 1815, stood in the Rue des Cendres, on the site of what is now a very large Hospital. I went there, and was admitted without difficulty. The Nursing Sister pointed out to me what remains of the Duke's house, this surviving portion being occupied by the nurses of the hospital. *I observed through the open windows that the ceilings were ornamental ; and such as would not be placed in hospital rooms.* In the yard, or neglected garden, between this building and the lofty boundary wall, are a small mortuary chapel, and several non-descript buildings ; none of them of any great age. After a careful survey of the premises, I observed a lofty building, in apparent contact with the boundary wall of the hospital. Asking the Sister what this building was, she replied, the Brewery of the Rue de la Blanchisserie. My hopes were at once raised. Leaving the Hospital, I descended the Rue des Cendres ; and entered the Rue de la Blanchisserie at a very sharp turn to my left. I was at once shown into the office of the proprietor of the brewery. He knew nothing of any ball having taken place ; and there were certainly no visible signs of a ball-room from the outside, nor the inside, of his house. After some conversation, in which not the slightest hint was given by me of Lady de Ros's information, I asked the proprietor if he happened to know of whom his father had purchased the premises. He replied, "Certainly; of a coachbuilder, named Van Asch." I asked whether this coachbuilder had a depôt. "Yes, a very large one ; it is now my granary." "Can you show it to me?" "With pleasure: at this time of year it is, of course, empty." We then ascended about twelve steps *to the entresol*, and I found myself in the long-sought room. Immediately opposite to the door of entrance are windows, of which the light has been almost completely blocked by the wall of the hospital yard which I had just left. I may say here that neither the Duke of Brunswick, nor any other guest, could have sat in a niche; for, although the windows are numerous, and deeply sunk in the wall, the lower edge of each recess is 5 ft. from the floor. On returning to my hotel I at once wrote a letter to Lady de Ros. I asked no questions in it, for I required no further confirmation. My motive in writing was that I thought that Lady de Ros would be, of all people, the most pleased at the discovery of the room which she and others had sought in vain. I did not receive any reply from her until she had read my published letter addressed to "The Times" from Homburg [as printed above]. In her reply there is not the slightest denial of the essential facts. With the three particulars demurred to, in my opinion unimportant, I will now deal. First, that the room was not in the rear of the Duke of Richmond's house. To this I reply that, supposing that the house faced towards the

Y

boulevard, I stated that the room was in its rear ; but as I have now no doubt that the principal front of the house was towards the Rue des Cendres, this would put the room in its right position, at the side, according to Lady de Ros. The second objection is that the dimensions given by me are larger than those of the ball-room described by her. I should suppose that, from the period when balls were first given, no young lady has ever measured the room in which she danced : a room full, or half full, of people appears much smaller than when empty. The third objection strengthens my case. It is that the ball-room was on the ground floor ; and not on the first floor. The level of the Rue de la Blanchisserie is below that of the Rue des Cendres : and, taking the few outside steps of No. 40 and the twelve additional steps leading to the ball-room, the precise level of the Hospital yard is reached ; from this an easy access to the ball-room no doubt existed. That there should be such a marvellous series of coincidences as I have related seems to have struck Lady de Ros as difficult to account for ; she suggests, however, that " probably the present Rue de la Blanchisserie has been *rebuilt* since then."

To this very improbable theory I have two good

answers : first, the room is ancient ; more than 100 years old ; it is supported by many strong square wooden posts ; they have never been painted. The only room that I have ever seen that closely resembled it is the " Lower School " at Eton, immediately beneath " Long Chamber." It reminded me of this at once. The Rue de la Blanchisserie itself, so far from having been recently rebuilt, is an old-fashioned, and partially worn out street, that has seen better days.

I may be permitted to say that I am in the habit of weighing evidence, and balancing facts carefully ; and I think that most of your readers will come to the same conclusion as myself.

No doubt Lord and Lady De Ros, who did not see the room, which certainly existed at the time of their visit, a fact proving that their search was not exhaustive, were convinced by those who, knowing that the Duke of Richmond's house had been removed, honestly believed that the ball-room had gone with it : in fact Lady de Ros, in her letter to me, says that they accepted the dictum of "an old inhabitant." Old age does not always bring wisdom, and the oldest inhabitant may be as fallible as the youngest.

To prove anything absolutely is difficult.

We have all read, or heard of Archbishop Whateley's

"Historic Doubts as to the Existence of Napoleon
Bonaparte"; and the inscription which I have read
on the monument of Descartes, "I think; therefore
I am," is certainly not logical. I believe, however,
that the careful consideration of the above facts will
convince those interested in the matter that my conclusion is sound.

Lord Byron, turning aside from the melancholy
metaphysics in which he so frequently indulged,
astonished the world by his most magnificent apostrophe; and penned lines that will always thrill British
hearts. The most prominent cause of the doubts as
to the locality of the ball arose from the unscrupulous
æstheticism of our great painter Turner. Observing a
picturesque building, which still exists in the neighbourhood of the Hôtel de Ville, he illustrated Byron's
description by depicting the ball as taking place in
what was once, as it is said, the Duke of Alva's
residence.

[I found on returning to England that Finden, the
Engraver, had imitated Turner, who was not, in this
case, to blame: as regards what follows Turner was
guilty.]

In the "Pleasures of Hope" he represents, in a
beautiful vignette, the line—

" On Prague's proud arch the fires of ruin glow,"

not as at Praga, the suburb of Warsaw ; but Prague, the capital of Bohemia.

Another good reason for the losing sight of the ball-room is that it is, and has long been, completely masked by the houses of the Rue de Blanchisserie, and by the wall of the Hospital.

One incident in relation to Genappe may interest your readers. I have in my possession a splendid sword that was taken there by the Prussians from Napoleon's carriage, on the evening of Waterloo. The history of the sword is, I should say, unrivalled. It belonged originally to Mourad Bey, the Chief of the Mamelukes ; it was surrendered by him, in the midst of a fierce action in Egypt, to Murat, afterwards King of Naples, and is depicted in a large painting by Gros at Versailles ; the sword was given by Murat to Napoleon Bonaparte. When the latter met the Directory, on his sudden return from Egypt, not wishing to frighten them, he wore plain clothes ; but over them this beautiful sabre, as stated in Ireland's " Life of Napoleon." Intending, no doubt, that it should adorn his triumphant entry into Brussels, the Emperor had it in his carriage at Waterloo. Prince

Blucher presented it soon afterwards to the Duke of
Wellington; by him it was given to Lord Anglesey,
who commanded the Cavalry; and by him to my
father, his A.D.C. during the Campaign. The sword
has a repoussé silver-gilt scabbard; and the blade,
which is as sharp as when wielded by Mourad Bey,
has jewels set in the upper part.

You would not thank me for prolonging this letter
by a disquisition on the Campaign of Waterloo. You
may, however, permit me to express my surprize that,
among the numerous Historians who have written on
the subject, none have dwelt sufficiently upon the
prudence of the Duke of Wellington in sanctioning,
and probably suggesting, the Ball. It was of great
importance that the inhabitants of Brussels should
not know the precise time of the inevitable crisis.
The sympathies of many of them were strongly in
favour of the French. Had the slightest émeute
taken place in Brussels, the news would have been
carried, with exaggeration, by Napoleon's spies, of
whom the town was full, to the French camp; and
would, of course, have given his troops the greatest
encouragement. The nonsensical theory that the
Duke was surprized has long passed away. He previously marked with his thumbnail on the Duke of

Richmond's map the precise spot on which Waterloo was fought; and he expressed his wish to such Officers as had been invited, not a numerous body, that they should attend the ball.

Unreasoning persons have called the Duke of Wellington a hard man, because he was a firm one. Clear in his views, and unflinching in the execution, of his duty, he showed on numerous occasions that his nature was gentle. Not only did he shed abundant tears when the list of his friends who had fallen in the Great Battle was read to him; but his conduct on the day after was that of one who felt the deepest grief. I know, from one who stood by, what occurred. On the morning after Waterloo some young ladies met him in Brussels; and naturally welcomed him with enthusiastic delight: he had defeated the day before the great conqueror; and, with inferior forces, he had won, as he above all others well knew, a Victory the most decisive in its effects that the World has ever known. The Hero turned away from these congratulations: and in a tearful voice replied, "No, no: it has been bought very dearly, I assure you."

Your obedient servant,

WILLIAM FRASER.

Homburg. Sept. 3.

The following reply from **Lord de Ros** appeared in " THE TIMES" of Sept. 13.

THE WATERLOO BALL.

TO THE EDITOR OF THE TIMES.

" SIR,—As the statement made by Sir William Fraser regarding the supposed discovery of the room in which the ball given by the Duchess of Richmond on the 15th of June, 1815, took place has given rise to much correspondence, I desire to state that my mother has distinct recollections connected with this subject. She assures me that the room in which the ball took place was on the ground floor, and that its size does not by any means correspond with the dimensions of the room which Sir William Fraser has discovered; this is further proved by a ground plan of the Duke of Richmond's house in my mother's possession.

" When in Brussels in 1868 every possible effort was made by my mother to trace out the house in which the Duke of Richmond lived, without success. I therefore think that the conclusions drawn by Sir William Fraser must be erroneous.

" This may appear a trifling matter, but as it may affect future history I venture to send you these few remarks, more particularly as I am anxious to put an end to the annoyance caused to my mother in her 93rd year by the unnecessary amount of correspondence which has been forced upon her in consequence of allusion having been made to her presence at the ball.

"I have the honour to be, Sir, your obedient servant,

"DE ROS.

"Old Court, Strangford."

I will only say that there was no allusion in my first letter that pointed to Lady de Ros, if this be the meaning of the expressions used: I most thoughtfully, and carefully worded it so that the public should not know to whom I referred: all that I said might have been given to me by my cousin, Lady D., who, as Miss Craufurd, appears with her father and mother in the list of those present at the Ball. Lady de Ros's personal communication, in her own name, to the "Daily Telegraph," compelled me to mention her in my reply. In her letter to me Lady de Ros expressed doubts as to whether my allusion was to herself.

"The Times" containing Lord de Ros's letter reached Interlaken on the evening of the 15th of September. I had *the day before* posted the following:

THE WATERLOO BALL.

To the Editor of The Times.

Sir,—I have to-day read the letter in "The Times" of the 11th inst. The quotations confirm the statement made by me in the letter which you did me the honour to insert on August 25. That statement covers, I think, the whole argument on the question. The facts being admitted that I was told by a lady in whose father's house the ball was given, and who was present herself, that it did not take place in the house, but in a coachmaker's depôt closely adjacent; that this coachmaker's depôt was in 1815, in the Rue de la Blanchisserie; that, after visiting what remains of the Duke of Richmond's house, I should, without any intimation that I was seeking for a coachmaker's depôt, be shown into one precisely on the spot indicated, touching the Duke of Richmond's house on one side, and placed in the old Rue de la Blanchisserie, still bearing the same name, seems to me an incontestable proof that the ball of June 15, 1815, the night before Quatre Bras, must have been given at No. 40 in the street named, and nowhere else.

Various places have been shown at different times in Brussels, without any authority, for the simple purpose of obtaining money from travellers. I have within the last few days met two gentlemen, not known to each other, Sir Albert Rollit, and the Rev. Teignmouth Shore, who have added their confirmation. Sir Albert Rollit told me that eight or ten years ago he presided at a lecture given at Hull by Lord William Lennox on "Wellington." Sir Albert does not recollect whether he introduced the circumstances of the ball, in his lecture; but he perfectly remembers that, in the course of a long conversation after it, Lord William, who was, I believe, staying in his house at the time, said that the ball given by the Duchess of Richmond, his mother, was not in the Hôtel de Ville, as sometimes shown; but in a room *adjacent* to his father's house.

The Rev. Teignmouth Shore writes to me:

"Some years ago I was going to Brussels; and spoke to my friend Lord William Pitt Lennox as to the ball which his mother had given, and at which he had been present; and inquired could he give me any indication as to where the house was; as I had on other occasions failed to find it. He told me that the house no longer existed; but that in any case the *Ball had not taken place at the residence of the Duchess; but in some sort of an old barn at the back of behind* [printed in error '*or*']. This rough-and-ready description seems to correspond with your view; and to confirm its truth."

In all cases there are persons inclined to doubt and disbelieve, however precise the evidence. In this matter the arguments against the identity of the room have been very feeble. As I stated in my letter to you, the locality has been hunted for during the last fifty years repeatedly; and without success. Had the *investigations been thorough, the room, of which I have written, and have seen, would certainly have been found.* It was not found by those who accepted, without proof, the statement of the inhabitants that the ball-had gone with the house.

That there should be two Coachmakers' Depôts, each touching the Duke of Richmond's late house, and each situated in the Rue de la Blanchisserie, would be a most marvellous coincidence. This, however, is physically impossible, for there is not space enough between the Rue des Cendres and the street named for another room capable of holding 200 guests; about the number invited.

The dancing took place, no doubt, in the old-fashioned pillared room described. The probabilities are that the supper-room, and other apartments necessary for a ball, were in the mansion itself, with which there was communication.

The ball-room has been masked, I might say buried, by the wall of the Hospital on one side, and by the houses of the Rue de la Blanchisserie on the other. The latter is an old, and somewhat worn-out street.

The Duke of Wellington, remarking on Incredulity, which is, I think, a greater indication of feeble reasoning powers than its converse, used to say that he had read more than once that he could not possibly have been present in person at the battle of Quatre Bras; adding, "However, I never found that they could explain away the 25,000 men who fought there under my orders."

Your obedient servant,

WILLIAM FRASER.

Interlaken. Sept. 14.

The following letter appeared on Dec. 10.

THE WATERLOO BALL.

To the Editor of The Times.

SIR,—I have been unwilling to trouble you on the

above subject, until I was in possession of some new facts.

Since my return to England, a few days ago, I have ascertained that in 1815 no other Coachmaker's Depôt existed in the Rue de la Blanchisserie, except that at No. 40, in which the ball took place. In "Bruxelles à travers les Ages" M. Hyman, the author, states in vol. ii. that the historical ball was given by the Duchess of Richmond in the Rue de la Blanchisserie.

The Rue de la Blanchisserie existed in 1815 ; it existed in 1868 ; and it exists now. It is a long, narrow, old street ; *it has always borne its present name.*

As regards the plan spoken of, it has never been compared with the room. The plan of a house nearly demolished cannot be of much value ; and, as it is admitted that the ball did not take place in the house, it appears to be worthless.

I am glad to hear that there are daily visitors to the scene of the ball.

Your obedient servant,

December 7.   WILLIAM FRASER.

On the 8th of December the following article was published by Mr Richard Edgcumbe, whose researches in

relation to **Lord** Byron are well known : I have **not**
the honour of his acquaintance : **nor have I had any**
communication with him, direct, nor indirect.

" Shortly after the appearance of Sir William
Fraser's very straightforward, **and, to my mind,** con-
vincing letter, a lady wrote to 'The Times,' and
pointed out that ' Notes and Queries,' 4ᵗʰ S. iii. **261,**
[*in the year 1869,*] contained a note by Mʳ C. W.
Bingham, which runs as follows :

" ' I had a recent opportunity of inquiring of a person, **than** whom none was more likely to be informed,
and although he could **not give me the number of**
the house, he appeared to **me to identify it with that**
in the **Rue des Cendres.** He said it was in a small
street near the Jardin Botanique, and leading out of
the **Rue de la Blanchisserie ; and** added that the
room in which the ball was given was the *gallery of a
late coachbuilder's shop*, thus rather destroying the
illusion **of**

" The window'd niche of **that high hall." '**

" In April, 1884, I approached Lady De Ros through
the **Duke of Richmond, with a** view to settling once
and for ever two very difficult Byronic points. I had,

of course, like every other gaping tourist, been shown the 'Salle de Reception' in the Hôtel de Ville at Brussels, where, according to those pests, the town guides, I had been assured that the Duke of Brunswick's 'prophetic ear' had caught the sound of his own doom. And yet I was not happy. Feeling sure that the Duchess of Richmond would not have given a ball in the Hôtel de Ville, I determined to apply to a lady who was actually present on that occasion. On April 9, 1884, Lady De Ros very kindly wrote down the following words, which I shall treasure all my life long:

"'The ball given by my mother the Duchess of Richmond, 15 June, 1815, took place in the Rue de la Blanchisserie, where we lived, in the lower part of the town of Bruxelles. There was no park attached to it, but a moderate-sized garden. The house had belonged to a coachmaker, and *the warehouse in which he kept his carriages was converted into a long narrow room, in which the ball took place.* In 1868 I looked in vain for the house *and the street,* and, after many inquiries, *was told* that the house had been pulled down, and *the street no longer existed,* or if it did its name was changed.

"'GEORGIANA DE ROS.'

"It further appears, by the evidence of Lord William Pitt Lennox, published by Sir William Fraser in 'The Times' (September 18), that the ball which his mother had given, and at which he was present, did '*not* take place at the residence of the Duchess, but *in some sort of an old barn at the back of behind.*' Thus it will be seen that the theory of Sir William Fraser is borne out by strong contemporary evidence. I congratulate him on having made the discovery; and on settling a point which has perplexed us long.

" RICHARD EDGCUMBE.

" 33 Tedworth Square, S.W."

The excellent plate of the Ball-room appeared in "The Graphic": it was done without my knowledge: Dr Lewis Jones, of 6 West Street, Finsbury Circus, from whose admirable photograph the plate is taken, has kindly permitted me to reproduce it in this volume: I have to thank him, and the Editor of "The Graphic" for their courtesy.

I believe that the case which I have put will, if carefully considered, be held to be conclusive that the Ball was held in the granary of Nos. 40 and 42 Rue de la Blanchisserie.

THE CONCURRENCE OF TESTIMONY of ab-
solutely disinterested persons cannot in my opinion be
gainsaid. I have, however, a witness whom I can
place in the box, not anticipated, that will strengthen,
if there be any necessity of strengthening, my case; and
whose evidence is, as the reader will admit, irresistible.

It is this: *The rooms shown by Lady de Ros in
the plan published by her last January, as existing in
1815, exist at this moment.* I have reproduced here
an absolute facsimile of the plan published by Lady
de Ros. I ask the reader either to take this volume,
or, if more convenient, to trace carefully, and exactly,
the plan of the ground floor of the Duke of Richmond's
house published by Lady de Ros, and reproduced
here. Let him desire the driver of his hired carriage
to take him to the Rue de la Blanchisserie. Let him
ascertain whether the street exists now. Let him
observe the length of the street: then let him enter
the Hospital in the Rue des Cendres; and place
himself at the point A. Let him observe the stone
steps into the house. Let him look into the room on
his left, marked B. If not permitted to enter, he can
judge of the size, as I did, from the outside. He will
be able to form a sound opinion as to whether a room,
of the size which he will see, could have held the 220

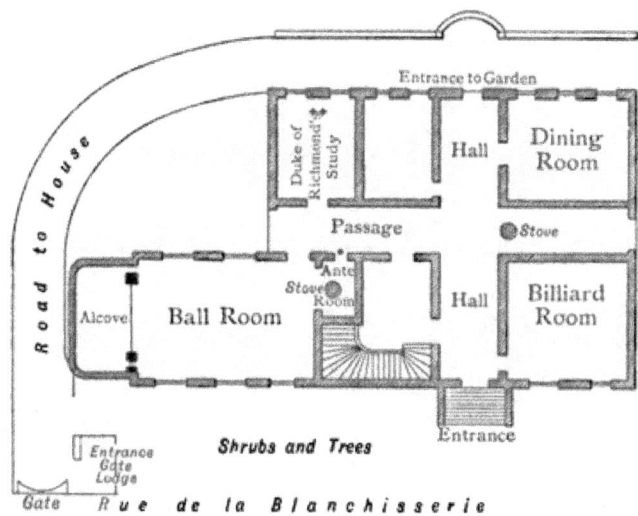

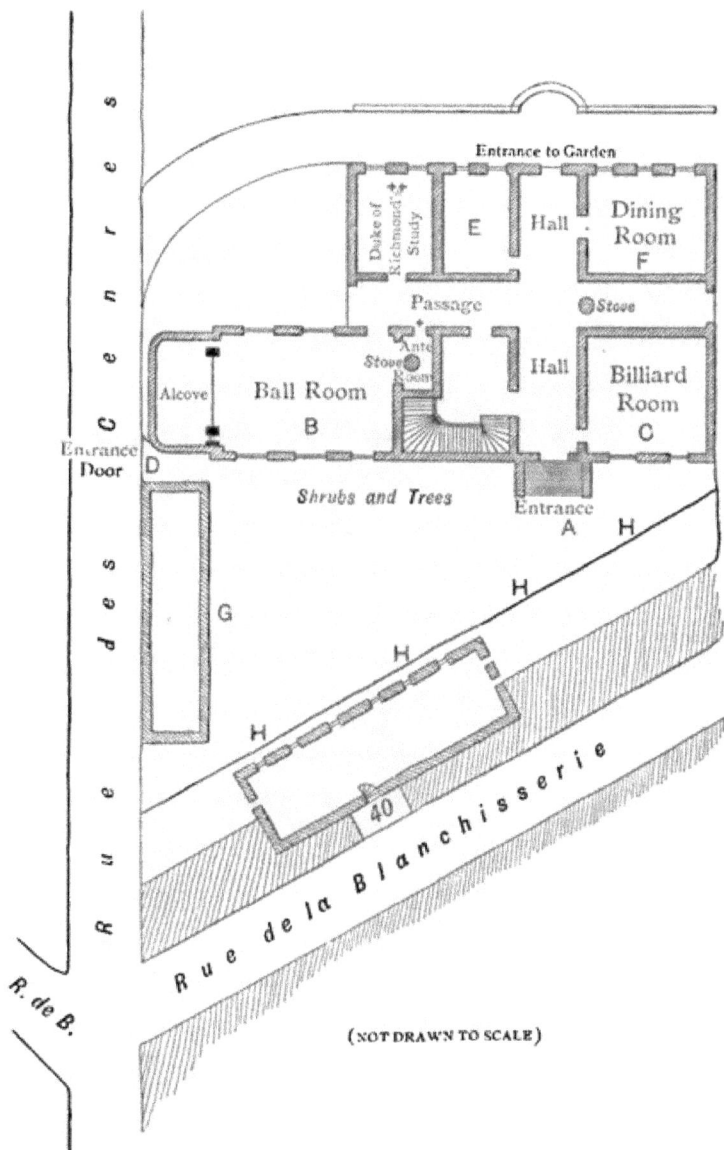

Rue des Cenres

R. de B.

Entrance to Garden

Duke of Richmond Study

E

Hall

Dining Room
F

Passage

Stove

Alcove

Ball Room
B

Ante Room
Stove

Hall

Billiard Room
C

Entrance Door
D

Shrubs and Trees

Entrance
A

H

H

G

H

H

H

Rue de la Blanchisserie

40

(NOT DRAWN TO SCALE)

persons named, with the musicians, servants, and probably other guests, whose names do not appear. Of the rooms beyond, E. F., I have no knowledge : but these two rooms B. C. I saw distinctly. Let the intelligent reader form his own opinion as to whether the room is not an ordinary, ornamental, dwelling-room of a by no means large house. Let him judge for himself whether the room marked in Lady de Ros's plan 'Ball-room' answers to her description written to Mr Richard Edgcumbe on April 9, 1884, p. 336 : "The warehouse, in which he (the coach-maker) kept his carriages, was converted into a long, narrow room, in which the ball took place:" or to Lord William Lennox's description of a "sort of old barn, at the back of behind."

Having done this, let him observe the lofty wall H. H. behind him. Let him look at the tiled roof, which appears above, which attracted my attention (C. is a Chapel recently built): having done this, let him leave the Hospital, not forgetting the poor-box of the excellent Sisters ; and, des-cending the Rue des Cendres, marked C., formerly the carriage road to the garden front of the house, let him ascend the left division of the Rue de la Blanchisserie, carefully noting the *space* between

the Hospital and the Rue de la Blanchisserie. Let
him pay a visit to the granary of Monsieur and
Madame Vanginderachter, at Nos. 40, 42, where he
will be received with courtesy ; and let him enter the
" long, low, narrow, room," that was Mr Van Asch's,
the coachmaker's, depôt : let him, after consideration,
decide in his own mind whether, had Lord William
Lennox written volumes on the subject, he could
have given a more accurate, and precise description
of the room, than when he said " The Ball was not
in my father's house ; but in a sort of old barn at the
back of behind." Let the visitor particularly observe
how the windows have been completely darkened by
the lofty wall built for the seclusion of the Hospital.
He will, I think, come to the conclusion that in a
family proverbial for hospitality, the room B. was
frequently the scene of dancing, and festivity ; but
that on this particular evening the Duke of Richmond
inviting a very large number, certainly far more than
he would on an ordinary occasion, did what a sensible
man would do under the circumstances ; namely hired
this old empty room ; and that he and the Duchess
entertained their guests in an apartment which,
although now not dignified except by age, was, no
doubt, decorated for the night ; and made sublime

by those who were present ; and by the circumstances under which the Ball was given.

The addition which I have made to Lady de Ros's plan *is not drawn ' to Scale'* : it is merely intended to convey my recollection of the locality. Had the same *proportions* been observed as in Lady de Ros's plan there would not, of course, have been room for it in the page.

FOR ONE REASON I might wish that the room which Lady de Ros has pointed out, and which now exists, might be the scene of the Ball: it is this : the Rue de la Blanchisserie is, as I have said, an old street. It may very possibly follow the destiny of old streets, which debouch on a fashionable quarter. Its Brewery, and its shops may be removed ; and replaced by a Street of Palaces. The present Proprietors of 40 and 42, are, I believe, soon about to retire upon their wealth. No one can tell what may be the fate of the old ' carriage depôt ' ; now a granary ; and for one immortal night a ball-room : whereas, the small room indicated in Lady de Ros's plan will, we may well assume, as part of a new, substantial, and flourishing Institution remain in its present condition for many generations.

I am quite incapable of permitting such a non-sensical idea to enter my head as to wish for a monopoly of the ball-room.

In any case, what the Italians call ' La poca Gloria ' will be mine.

Half a century of investigation having failed to find the room, I may claim some little credit in having done so; whether the ball was given in the granary, or whether it was given in one of the private rooms of the Hospital. That the room *exists at this moment* is a fact which certainly no one knew before the month of August 1888. I did my best in 1884 to enable Colonel Montague to find the ball-room.

I told Mr Vanginderachter that I would not repay his courtesy in showing me the ball-room by attracting attention to it; as this might involve him in a good deal of trouble from persons who wished to gain admission. I said that there was one person that I should probably see at Homburg who, I felt sure, would be interested in the matter, and whom I should like to tell. He at once said that I need have no scruples on the subject; gave me several of his cards; and expressed most cordially his willingness to show the room to anyone who chose to come.

I HAVE, in writing this volume, wished to give only my own recollections of the Duke, and facts related to me by those whom I considered excellent authorities. Had I written all the stories that I could remember, I could have added for each one told at the least two : had I referred to the many works already published relating to him, I could of course have increased this number almost without limit.

In cases where I have referred to relations already in print, it has been with a view to correct them.

The lines in rhyme or blank that are not between inverted commas are not quotations.

I HAVE TAKEN from the book-shelves of my brain the volumes 'WELLINGTON,' and 'WATERLOO' : the reader has the result.

THE MORE deeply, and thoroughly, we examine the Duke's character, the more we admire it.

To those who have the fatal gift of idealization such a character as the Duke of Wellington's offers Repose. For once they find their Ideal exists.

To those who have the sad talent of minute, and

perspicuous observation, the Duke's conduct is also satisfactory.

To those, and they are but few, who have the misfortune to possess both these qualities; who 'walk in a region that they find almost uninhabited'; it is a consolation to believe that Human Nature has for once reached such perfection.

This Globe has produced three beings, whose names will only perish when the Earth itself shall be dissolved into its elements; a POET, an ARTIST, and a MAN: of these BRITAIN claims two; ITALY one: SHAKESPEARE the POET; MICHAEL ANGELO the ARTIST; WELLINGTON the MAN.

INDEX.

www.ingramcontent.com/pod-product-compliance
Lightning Source LLC
Chambersburg PA
CBHW030916270326

41929CB00008B/721